A Wiser Guy

Louis P DiVita

A WISER GUY

Copyright © 2014 by Louis P DiVita

All rights reserved. No part of this publication may be reproduced, distributed, or transmitted in any form or by any means, including photocopying, recording, or other electronic or mechanical methods, without the prior written permission of the author, except in the case of brief quotations embodied in critical reviews and certain other noncommercial uses permitted by copyright law.

ISBN 978-0-9970363-0-5 (paperback)
ISBN 978-0-9970363-1-2 (hardcover)

Cover designed by Louis P DiVita and Jonathan Schwark

www.awiserguy.com

Dedicated

To all my family, friends, associates and adversaries who played starring, co-starring or supporting roles in my life, enabling me to be able to tell my story.

A special thank you to Big Elena, who said "Louis you know all the stories you need to write them down."

I opted to keep some stories sacred.

Acknowledgements

Art Demis for his continuing prodding to finish the book

Thomas Hunt for introducing me to Mike Tona

Mike Tona for sharing his years of research which validated many of my stories

Lizabeth Felti for working as editor and creative consultant

Jonathan Schwark for his friendship and technical support in the cover design, web site and trailer

Jamie Lesher for his friendship and support

The miracle of the internet

Joe Leon for his talent

Peter Upton for his Invaluable help

George Catalano for sharing his connections

The Buffalo Bill Bountiful Table Project

Benedetto Angelo Palmeri's obituary told of his notoriety. But, like the men in his world, the public never hears of the good. We are grateful to the Buffalo Evening News that in December 1932, in the subtitle of his obituary, wrote "Was Benefactor of Italian Colony". The obituary stated "He passed out $5s and $10s to tide his lowly friends until work became more available. To the citizens of the lower west side he was their individual welfare department, a man who could and would aid them when pride kept them from appealing to the organized charities Especially grateful were the members of upwards of a score of families whose only source of food each Christmas for years had been Angelo B. Palmeri." While not as notorious, his brother, Paul, and his sister, in law Elena, my grandparents were also active helping the less fortunate. Our family has continued to honor their legacy and help the less fortunate in any way that we can. Writing this book and telling the stories would not be complete unless a portion of the proceeds were designated to helping others in need. Through the "Buffalo Bill Bountiful Table Project," we will make a donation for every book purchased to the local food bank in the zip code of purchase. If you acquired this book via any means other than purchase, please help us and make a donation to your local food bank and benefit your less fortunate neighbors.

Contents

The Characters 1
Places 7
Investigations 8
The Buzzard, The Turtle and The Rabbit 9
Introduction 12
The Life 15
My First Communion 23
Papa 27
Improper Activities In The Labor Field 12315 29
Papa's Funeral 32
Before Papa Died 36
Christmas Eve With Santa 37
Not So Cute 39
I Heard There Was A Pot On 40
Grooming 41
Breaking Bread 43
Winky Dink 45
Papa's Temper 47
Papa's Status & Influence 50
Mr. Pepetone 52
After Papa Died 58
The Walk To Mama's 60
The Last Big Family Christmas 63
"Papa" & "Mama" 65
Mama Said 67
Mama 68
Mama's Stories 70
Breakfast With Mama 72
Goodfella 74
Mama Said Be A Pharmacist 75

Papa & Mama's Early Years	77
Buffalo Bill	78
Buffalo Bill Was A Character	80
Papa Was A Gambler	87
Papa & The Funeral Home	88
Mama Heard: St. Valentine's Day Massacre	89
Papa's Friends	91
Niagara Falls	96
New Jersey Rocks	98
Under One Roof	99
The Last Envelope	100
The Queen	102
Connections	103
One Of The Boys	104
Castellammarese War	105
Wild West	107
Mob Culture	108
Generosity	111
Goombada Willie	115
Dr. Morici & The Kefauver Hearings	117
Willie's Catholic Funeral	118
The Deal House	121
Moe Brown	123
Jimmy Guido	125
Easy Time	126
The Family	128
Mom	129
Dad	131
Dad & The Chinamen	132
The DiVitas	133
1955 World Series	137
Lucille Ball	138
Aunt Marie & Uncle Ange	140
Uncle Don	142
Uncle Ernie	145
Young Ernie	146
The Hustler	149
The La Salle	150
The Little Guy	151
Ernie's Reputation	152

Accident At The Fountain	154
Cadillac Ernie	155
The Wire Room	157
The Luncheonette	159
The Pink Elephant	161
Going Legit	162
Wayne, New Jersey	163
Ernie's Downfall	165
Give A Man A Fish	168
Uncle Frank	169
Poly Clean	170
Frank Sinatra	172
Who Married Who	173
Big Fight At Club 82	175
Lou Lou	176
Louis DiVita And Paul Palmeri	177
Macy's Thanksgiving Parade	178
Rockefeller Center Tree	180
The Bike Accident	181
Fair Lawn	182
My Friend Vinnie	183
My Other Cousin	185
Learning To Shoot	187
Crazy Stunts	189
Wanna Buy A Duck?	191
Earning	192
I Can Get It For You Wholesale	193
Englewood Golf And Country Club	196
Tony Bender	198
Ed Sullivan	200
Bernie Brillstein	202
School	204
Louis The Hairdresser	205
Beating The System	208
Accomplishments	209
From Cutting Hair To Cutting Grass	210
My First Collection	211
Ernie's Return	213
Riding With Ernie	214
Ol'Blue Eyes	216

Back When I Was Rich And Famous	217
Big Plans	218
Who's Sorry Now?	219
Rogers Peet	220
Sandi	221
Camelot	222
Bernard R Treich (aka Bernie, Bumpy, Boom Boom)	226
Supplemental Income	228
Always Grant An Accomodation	230
Houston: Boom Or Bust	232
Associated Industries	234
Selex	237
New Jersey Bound	241
Willowbrook Nissan	242
Garfield	244
Don't Trust Nobody — But You Can Trust Lou	247
Florida Trash & The Horseshit King	249
Mafia Wife	252
Perception	254
Franchising	257
Philly	258
Realization	260
Don't Fuck With Lou	261
The Art Of Collection	263
Louis's Temperament Barometer	266
Mr DiVita	269
Turning 50	270
A Different Road	271
Nono's Recipes	275

The Characters

Umberto (The Mad Hatter) Albert Anastasia — A founder of the American Mafia, Anastasia ran Murder, Inc. during the prewar era and was boss of the modern Gambino crime family during most of the 1950s.

Lucille Ball — An American actress, comedienne, executive and TV producer, she was the star of the sitcoms *I Love Lucy*, *The Lucy–Desi Comedy Hour*, *The Lucy Show*, *Here's Lucy*, and *Life with Lucy*.

Joey Bishop — An American comedian who appeared on television as early as 1948 and eventually starred in his own weekly comedy series. He was a member of the "Rat Pack" with Frank Sinatra, Peter Lawford, Sammy Davis Jr. and Dean Martin.

Bernard "Bernie" Brillstein — Film and television producer, executive producer and talent agent, He produced the TV Shows *Hee Haw*, *The Muppet Show*, *Saturday Night Live*, *News Radio*, *Just Shoot Me!*, *The Larry Sanders Show* and *The Sopranos*. He produced the movies The *Blues Brothers*, *Ghostbusters*, *Dragnet*, *Ghostbusters II*, *Happy Gilmore* and *The Cable Guy*.

Cassandro (Tony The Chief) Bonasera—A member of the Profaci Family and close Ally of the Palmieris.

Joseph (Joe the Barber) Barbara—Close associate of the Palmeris and Santo Volpe. Powerful in NY and became boss of Volpe/Bufalino family in northern Pennsylvania.

Rosario Alberto Russell Bufalino aka (McGee) and (The Old Man)—The boss of the Northeastern Pennsylvania crime family from 1959 to 1989. Started his career working for the Palmeris, then joined Santo Volpe in Pittston, PA.

Antonio (Tony) Canzoneri—Five time World Boxing Champion. He was a Capo in the Bonanno Family and, after retiring from the ring, bought a resort hotel in Newburgh, NY.

Francesco Castiglia (Frank "The Prime Minister") Costello— Boss of the Luciano/Genovese family who had close ties to the Palmeris.

Giovanni Ignazio Dioguardi (Johnny Dio)—A labor racketeer. He is known for the blinding of newspaper columnist Victor Riesel and creating fake labor union locals to help Jimmy Hoffa become General President of the Teamsters.

Giuseppe (Joe Adonis, "Joey A") Antonio Doto—A Palmeri friend, partner of Willie Moretti and a founding member of the post—Castellammarese war Mafia.

Frank Erickson—Arnold Rothstein's right-hand man and New York's largest bookmaker during the 1930s and 40s.

Thomas (Tommy Ryan) Eboli—New York City mobster who eventually became the acting boss of the Genovese crime family.

George A. Franconero—Brother of the singer Connie Francis, law partner of NJ Governor Brendan T. Byrne and later became a cooperating witness in several mob trials.

Vito (Don Vito) Genovese—Founding member of the post Castellammare War Mafia. Became leader of the Genovese crime family. He was known as Boss of all Bosses from 1957–1959.

Althea Gibson—Tennis player and professional golfer. First black athlete to cross the color line of international tennis. In 1956, she became the first person of color to win a Grand Slam title.

James (Jimmy, Uncle Bunny) Guido—Close friend of Dad's, Uncle Ernie and Uncle Frank. Successful home builder who lost his fortune but always reached for the brass ring.

Thomas Rocco Barbella (Rocky Graziano)—One of the greatest knockout artists in boxing history who displayed the capacity to take his opponents out with a single punch.

Buddy Hackett—Comedian and actor who purchased Albert Anastasia's house.

Salvatore Charles (Lucky Luciano) Lucania—Considered the father of modern organized crime for the establishment of the Commission. He was, for many years, the boss of the Lucania/ Genovese crime family.

Tony Manzella—Owner of the Pink Elephant Restaurant in Lodi NJ.

Stefano (Steve, The Undertaker) Magaddino—Dominant in the Buffalo underworld for fifty years. He was the longest tenured boss in the history of the American Mafia.

Salvatore Anthony (Sal the Barber) Maglie—Major League Baseball pitcher who He played from 1945 to 1958.

Salvatore Maranzano—From the town of Castellammare del Golfo, Sicily. He instigated the Castellammarese War and became the Mafia's short lived "Boss of Bosses".

Rocky Marciano (born Rocco Francis Marchegiano)—Undefeated World Heavyweight Champion. Marciano is the only person to hold the heavyweight title without a tie or defeat.

John C. Montana (born Giovanni Montana)—A Buffalo, New York labor racketeer, political fixer and elected politician who eventually became the Underboss and Consiglieri of the Buffalo crime family.

Dr.Theodore Morici—Chief surgeon at Beth Israel hospital, Passaic, NJ. Physician to numerous mob figures.

Miss Lyons—Dr Morici's nurse and trusted administrator.

Corbett Monica—Appeared with Frank Sinatra so often he became a junior member of the Rat Pack. He later became Joey Bishop's sidekick, friend and manager on *The Joey Bishop Show*

Robert Francis "Bobby" Kennedy—Brother of President John F Kennedy. He gained national attention as the chief counsel of the Senate Labor Rackets Committee from 1957 to 1959.

Peter (Lodi Pete) Laplaca—Uncle Don's father who was Willie Moretti's driver, body guard and successor as Boss of NJ.

(Tony Pro) Provenzano—A Capo in the Genovese family and vice president of Teamsters Local 560. He was connected to Jimmy Hoffa and President Richard Nixon.

Giuseppe (Pepe) Sabato—Subordinate to Willie Moretti who rose to Capo in the Genovese family.

Anthony (Tony) Scoma—A northern New Jersey Genovese associate who delivered weekly payments to Mama.

Anthony M. Scotto—Head of ILA local 1814, International Longshoremen's Association. Achieved a high level of influence with several New York mayors, U.S. Attorney General Robert Kennedy, Governor Hugh Carey, Mario Cuomo and Jimmy Carter.

Frank (Moe Brown) Sesta—Close friend of Dad, Uncle Ernie and Uncle Frank. Came up under Willie Moretti and operated on the fringes of organized crime

Anthony C. (Tony Bender) Strollo—A New York mobster who served as a high ranking Capo of the Genovese crime family for several decades.

Ed Sullivan—American television personality, sports and entertainment reporter and syndicated columnist for the *New York Daily News*. Host of The *Ed Sullivan Show*, the longest-running variety show in US broadcast history.

Glenn Teal—PGA Pro Golfer and club pro Englewood Golf and Country Club.

Ralph Terry—Right-handed pitcher for the NY Yankees and MVP of the 1962 World Series.

Jerry Volpe—Owner and club pro at the Englewood Golf and Country Club.

Santo Volpe—A close ally of the Palmeris. In addition to his work as president of a coal company, he led a Mafia organization known as the Men of Montedoro in the Northern Pennsylvania mining communities.

Places

Englewood Golf Club — A golf course located in Englewood and Leonia, New Jersey, just outside New York City. It hosted the U.S. Open in 1909.

"The Games" AKA The Lodi Garage — Bill Miller's Rivera (Gambling Dens, Dice Barns) owned and operated by Joe Adonis and Willie Moretti.

"The Wire Room" — The operations center for the New York metropolitan area mob book making operations.

82 Club — From 1958-1978, it was a legendary drag cabaret located on the southwest corner of 4th St. and 2nd Avenue. Ty Bennett becomes the headliner and "den mother." A favorite hangout of Harvey Fierstein, 82 Club makes cameo appearances in both Torch Song Trilogy and The Rose. By the 1960s and 70s, 82 Club became a popular hangout for celebrities and glam rockers like David Bowie and Lou Reed. The Stilettos (the precursor to Blondie) and The New York Dolls performed there during this time.

The Pink Elephant — A Lodi, NJ Restaurant and bar that served excellent Italian food.

Investigations

Kefauver Committee—The United States Senate Special Committee to Investigate Crime in Interstate Commerce was a special committee of the United States Senate which existed from 1950 to 1951 and which investigated organized crime that crossed state borders in the United States. The committee became popularly known as the Kefauver Committee because of its chairman, Senator Estes Kefauver.

McClellan Hearings—The McClellan hearings investigated organized Crime activities across America and investigated leading Mafia Figures of the era. The hearings were initiated by Arkansas Senator John L. McClellan.

The Buzzard, The Turtle and The Rabbit

This was one of Uncle Ernie's favorite jokes and kinda sums up my life. It has been said life imitates art and art imitates life. For me, being strong, capable and always wanting to please, summarizes how, during my life, I was seemingly relegated to the hard and lousy work, while others prospered.

A buzzard, a turtle and a rabbit were best friends. When it was time for them to leave their families and go out into the world, they tossed their belongings into a wheelbarrow and set out on their way. They happened upon a farmer who offered them work and paid them with an assortment of vegetable seeds. They worked for the farmer in exchange for the seeds, and when their work was finished, they tossed their seeds into the wheelbarrow and headed across the land, still wondering what fate held in store.

The very next day, while travelling through a beautiful valley, they came across an unclaimed piece of land. They decided to stake a claim and farm the land, using the seeds they had earned on their last job.

The turtle said, "I'm pretty low to the ground and have sharp claws, so I can use my claws to plow the ground and make furrows for the vegetable seeds."

The buzzard said, "I can fly over the furrows, and drop the seeds into them." But they needed fertilizer, and the only one who could handle the wheelbarrow was the rabbit.

The buzzard and turtle took their belongings out of the wheelbarrow and the rabbit set out in search of fertilizer. The turtle plowed the ground and the buzzard flew over the furrows and dropped the seed into them, and they waited for the rabbit to return with his load of fertilizer.

Several hours passed and the rabbit hadn't returned with the fertilizer. The hours turned to days, and the days to weeks. The buzzard and the turtle gave up hope of seeing the rabbit again. They knew they would have to raise their vegetable crop without him.

One day, the rabbit came upon manure that caused the grass, flowers and trees to flourish as he had never seen before. He loaded his wheelbarrow with manure and started to head home. He realized that he was lost, However, and could never find his way home, if his very life depended on it.

Gloom and despair overcame the rabbit, when a wise old owl flew down from an oak tree and stood at his side. The rabbit told the owl of his predicament and asked the owl if he could help him find his way back to his friends. The owl asked the rabbit to describe the land where he had last seen his friends and the owl knew exactly where it was and gave the rabbit directions that would take him back.

As the rabbit rounded the last turn in the road, he picked up his pace and began pushing the wheelbarrow as fast as it would go, thinking they might have built a little shack and would be watching for him on the front porch. The rabbit came to a screeching halt. Instead of a shack in on the hillside, there stood a mansion. The rabbit stood there in total disbelief.

At the entrance to the estate, the wrought iron arch read "The Estate of Mr. Buzzard and Mr. Turtle".

The estate did indeed belong to the rabbit's old friends. The ground was rich in nutrients and needed no fertilizer after all. Their vegetables flourished beyond their wildest imaginations and they had become extremely wealthy over the year. The rabbit decided to go up to the mansion and find out what was going on. So he grabbed the wheelbarrow and pushed until he was within reach of the doorbell.

A butler answered the front door and asked, "How may I help you?" The rabbit replied, "I'm here to see the buzzard and the turtle."

The butler looked down his nose at the rabbit and replied that they preferred to have their names pronounced with the last syllable accentuated, so that it sounded more like Mr. Buzzard and Mr. Turtell.

"Mr. Buzzard is out in the yard, and Mr. Turtell is out by the well, and they wish to remain undisturbed for the remainder of the day."

Just as the butler was about to shut the door in the rabbit's face, the rabbit leapt over the wheelbarrow, grabbed the butler by the lapels, and said, "You go tell Mr. Buzzard who's out in the yard and Mr. Turtell who's out by the well, and that Mr. Rabbit is here with the shit!"

Introduction

A WISER GUY chronicles sixty plus years of life experiences, encounters and the ups and downs of Louis P DiVita, the grandson of Paul Palmeri who was the brother of Benedetto Angelo (Buffalo Bill) Palmeri. They were founding members of the post-Castellammerse War Mafia.

Louis chronicles his torment between following his ancestor's gangster life style or the path to white collar success. His earliest childhood memories of the family's history began at seven years old when he was tutored initially by his grandmother and then by his mother, father, uncles, family friends and acquaintances.

He profiles the colorful Buffalo Bill Palmeri, the founder of the Mafia in Buffalo/Niagara Falls. Buffalo Bill was a generous Robin Hood whose dark side was not to be tested.

Paul (Don Paulo) Palmeri was a handsome, suave businessman, undertaker, elocutioner, radio host, and political leader who in concert with his brother controlled the flow of liquor from Canada to most of the major U.S. markets during prohibition. He was mostly off the national watch list until after the failed Apalachin Meeting and the convening of the McClellan hearings, at which time he became a person of interest to Bobby Kennedy.

Many rising stars in the mob worked with or apprenticed with the Palmeri brothers. The Palmeris had all the standard rackets: gambling, prostitution, protection, loan sharking, narcotics, kidnapping and white slavery.

Ernest Palmeri (Uncle Ernie, Cadillac Ernie, The Little Guy), who through Teamsters local 945, Totowa, New Jersey, reigned supreme in the allocation of garbage hauling contracts for the entire state. He tutored Louis in numerous illicit activities and helped establish a skill set which Louis could and did recall numerous times for survival. Ernie was good hearted, funny and sinister.

The text follows Louis' development as an independent hustler constantly trying to escape his legacy as he attempts to earn a legitimate income in the automobile business, oil field equipment sales, and the trash and recycling industry. Setbacks and failures continually drew him back to illicit earnings. The story follows Louis in grammar school monitoring fundraising projects for the skim, working with Uncle Ernie as a young teen in a complex shoplifting operation, collecting for bookmakers in his late teens and launching into adulthood operating independently selling drugs, guns, porn (pre Beta Max and VCRs), running a shoplifting ring, loan sharking, protection and collections.

Louis reminisces about his associations with but not limited to: Albert Anastasia, Santo Volpe, Russell Bufalino, Anthony Bonasera, Tommy Eboli, Rocky Graziano, Ralph Terry, Joey Bishop, Buddy Hackett, Bernie Brillstein, Ed Sullivan, Frank Erickson and a host of other people and influences.

Louis illustrates how posture, image and associates can send a more powerful message than muscle and guns. Using a series of serious and comical stories of crime and a middle class life, Louis pieces together people, places, situations and encounters spanning from the golden age of the mob (1920s to 1980s) to the present.

The Life

I had the honor and privilege to have been born into a family that some would idolize or emulate due to the public's amazement, interest, and love affair with mobsters. As a child, teenager and young man, I myself was enamored by the gangster lifestyle, even though I had witnessed more rough times than good. Throughout my life, there was always a pulling, tugging and conflict in my brain. How did my family's values and teachings relate to my development as a man?

Anybody who has studied the mob lifestyle at any level thinks they can relate to the mindset of gangsters and those around them. Not so. Gangsters have difficulty distinguishing poverty versus wealth. In the movie *Donnie Brasco*, Lefty Ruggiero explains the honor of being a Wise Guy and brags about having 23 hits to his claim. But we see Lefty standing outside the crew's social club, waiting to pay homage to their captain. What man of honor? Especially in light of a scene showing Lefty breaking open parking meters for spending money and getting dressed down by his skipper for shallow earnings, with the general threat that if this continues, somebody's going to get clipped.

Many of my own personal experiences were with Made Guys and associates who did everything from hustle junk cars, costume jewelry, sweaters, and the like for, as we say, "Corks." (Corks is chump change.) If The Life was so great, why would they resort to this? Be clear, this was not swag from a holdup or the spoils of a hijacking. This was anything for a buck, because times were lean. The same guys trying to squeeze tens and twenties here and there were tipping bartenders 50 dollar bills. You see, sports betting, loansharking, extortion and all forms of racketeering didn't always pay off. Kind of here today, gone tomorrow.

One of the things I found most interesting was, while representing oneself as being a power player, these same men made no qualms about crying poverty. The dress, the car and the image went completely out the window when times got tough.

Myself, I am a student and the end result of the image, more than The Life. I could have zero in my pocket, but carried myself in a posture with confidence that would make you believe I had millions. I believe I was an A student. I not only excelled in my studies but was top of the class in practical application. I do believe that life is one big act or stage. Those who display strength, have strength. Those with finesse are admired and looked up to.

While I tried to acquire a comfortable existence and moderate wealth, my attempts were mostly in legitimate arenas. When times got tough or legitimacy did not work, I resorted to my gene pool and did whatever I had to do. With big scores comes big risk and massive penalties, with small scores (or as I like to call it, "supplemental income") risk is small. It's also a great way to get by when times get tough. I never degraded myself hustling costume jewelry, busting open parking meters, etc. I was in the new and used car business.

Most of what I did was legitimate, although during my career we did it all, from clocking (turning back speedometers,) doctoring transmissions and engines, washing titles, whatever it took.

Once again, it's how you carry and present yourself. If they really believe you come from the dark side, they believe the merchandise came from a heist. By operating on the fringes, knowing I could always get help if needed, dropping the right name at the right time... in my mind, in my world, I was in the best position possible.

People quietly questioned, "Who is this guy?" just enough to keep them guessing. It's been written and documented that most people in The Life have a front. The reason, many years ago, that the most powerful mobsters kept a low profile was it gave them opportunity to earn legitimately and illegitimately without heat or pressure. Once you became known by law enforcement, it became impossible to maintain the low profile.

If we go back to the Kefauver investigations of the early 1950s, Willie Moretti was identified as a gambler. Joe Adonis, Frank Costello, were both classified as gamblers. They all had arrest records; they all had been involved in bootlegging. (Public knowledge). But it was not until the 1960s and the McClellan hearings that the real power racketeers had over labor and many legitimate businesses was discovered.

You see, the ultimate goal of the Founding Fathers was legitimate business and no involvement for their sons and grandsons. As with any business or enterprise, there is always a newcomer who wants a better life, and for him it is hard work and toil. We've seen this in the evolution of sport—every ethnic group has had its day in the sun. Today it's dominated by blacks and Hispanics. As Apollo Creed said to Rocky, "You've got to have the eye of the tiger."

Unfortunately, the master plan of our forefathers failed for several reasons. Some of their associates, some older, some younger, were never satisfied, and the thirst for power overtook common sense and financial security.

The man most recognized for taking his dirty money and laundering it 'till sparkling clean was Joe Kennedy. It is my estimation, based on my knowledge of prohibition, that Mr. Kennedy could not have made more money than some of my ancestors and their closest allies. Mr. Kennedy used his winnings to enter the political arena, dignify himself, and install a son in the White House. Not only was he intelligent, crafty and shrewd, he also represented what the general population believed to be more like them. He did not speak with a foreign accent and Irish-Americans had already been through their cycle of the United States' persecution of Irish immigrants. He executed his plan masterfully!

My grandfather, Paolo (Paul) Palmeri emigrated from Sicily in 1909 and was a member of the Castellammarese clan. Many of Papa's friends and associates did succeed. Their sons or sons-in-law attended college. They brought legitimacy to the family. We, on the other hand, had a variety of reasons why our parents did not have college. My mother, who was way ahead of her time, would have gone to college, but the old-time mentality was women do not need college. Ironically, she did go to mortuary school to aid my grandfather gain independence with his funeral business.

Too much has been written about Cosa Nostra, the Mafia, Mobsters, etc. Most of the writings are redundant rhetoric by authors who read other people's writings. They have compiled information from books, newspapers and magazines. While some documentation and fact can be derived from these sources, nothing is better than first-hand information and eyewitness accounting.

If we go back in history, little was known about the Mob, Mafia, Cosa Nostra, whatever. The violence, bloodshed and their members' reputations as killers added to the public interest. After the Apalachian debacle and the McClellan investigations into labor racketeering (which exposed many people and their arrest records for total public consumption), Joe Valachi became the first known and much publicized Made Member to testify. He was given way more credit than he should have.

Common sense would tell us that he could not have been involved in and/or privy to all of the things he claimed. Like a writer, you can take a couple of pieces of information and embellish them into an elaborate story. His emphasis on structure, I believe, was over-exaggerated. Going back in time, there were several men recognized as heads of their families, but many who carried the title or designation of lowly soldiers had power and money far beyond many of their superiors.

According to the so-called experts, when Frank Costello abdicated the throne, he was a soldier. This I will dispute and mount a solid case to support what I know. In a well-run enterprise, this would not have been. In Valachi's words, and what is still believed, the workers could not possibly make more than the bosses, hence too much has been emphasized on structure.

While there was definitely a chain of command, I believe it was more structured within each small faction, crew, etc. than this whole tree structure. If it's true Costello was demoted to a lowly soldier, my claim about structure gains validity. A soldier would never be consulted by high ranking members and bosses such as Albert Anastasia, Carlo Gambino, Joe Bonanno, etc.

Joe Adonis was never identified as a member of any family, yet wielded huge power. The historians claim he was close to Albert Anastasia, yet he was partners with Willie Moretti in New Jersey, Meyer Lansky in Florida and very tight with Lucky Luciano. Go figure.

In the beginning, whatever your stature, there was not a major difference between your lifestyle and the so-called boss. Houses were similar, cars were similar, money in the pocket, food on the table, clothes on your back, and there was loyalty to each other. But just like the business world, greed will cause people to do strange things. Greater disparity between what the bosses and the workers had created dissension amongst the ranks, and, like any society, it caused coups.

Throughout my life, I encountered people, places and situations almost like it was planned. I open to you a look at a life touched in every way. Not another "How many guys I killed, beat up or robbed and oh by the way I'm sorry cause I'm broke story, but a real life interacting with the famous, infamous and average.

By the way, tell Rudy Giuliani et al they did not destroy organized crime as they claim. They disrupted the Italian faction, expanding the playing field for Russians, Asians and a host of other groups.

The 2000s have produced a new level of racketeers. They wear better suits, ride in limos, own numerous houses and have substantial assets. Oh yeah, their names end in vowels: Chase, Bank of America, Citi, and Wells Fargo

I was born into this world, These are my observations of family members and their associates, my real life experiences as a child, young adult, and fully grown man.

I remember everything in great detail, from the 1950's to today. Of course, I do not have first-hand information about what happened before I was born, but coming from the people who were there or heard from the participants directly, I think my account is about the next best.

I will reveal my personal experiences and the experiences of my grandfather, grandmother, parents, aunts, uncles and close and distant friends.

This is my story, written by me, in my own words. It took many years to get it all down on paper, but here it is.

On advice, I decided against using a "ghostwriter." I wrote the stories I felt I wanted to tell but by no means all the stories. To the best of my recollection, like it or not, this is the truth. I'm sure some people won't like my stories. You know what? FUCK EM!

May 7, 1955, Paul Palmeri died at Passaic General Hospital after a heart attack and short illness. He was 62. I took This Picture with My Kodak Brownie Camera

My First Communion

May 8, 1955, 7:00 AM

The steady drizzle and dark clouds caused an unseasonably chilly day and contributed to the somber and sorrowful mood all around me. Right fully so. As far as I was concerned, the whole world should be sad. After all, it is less than 24 hours since my world came to a screeching halt.

Papa died. *How God could let this happen period, let alone yesterday?*

I was dressed in my white First Communion suit and headed to St. Nicholas School to meet my classmates and take my place in the processional line to the church to receive my first Holy Communion. I made my first confession on Friday during school, so I was ready to receive my third sacrament in church on Sunday.

In the 1950's, you had to fast from midnight the night before you received Holy Communion. Hence, the early morning mass. I guess the priests, nuns and parents were concerned with the kids being too hungry if they did a later mass. In 1962, Pope John XXIII convened the Ecumenical Council in an attempt to retain membership and garner increased participation of the faithful.

Two major changes were: a one hour fast before communion, and you could now eat meat on Fridays, except during Lent.

There were two benefits of being Roman Catholic. First, you get out of school for church things. As boring as church is, it beats being in a classroom. Second, no matter what you did and how many sins you committed, you go to confession, say a few prayers (penance) and you're clean.

I don't recall having ever been up till midnight, except for New Year's Eve, but the night Papa died was unlike anything I'd ever known. Now it was early the next morning. Seven o'clock!

In church that dreary morning, I remember clutching my rosary beads, which I believed held holy powers. My mind was in and out as to what was happening around me. I was too preoccupied praying for and dedicating my first communion to Papa's soul. I knew he had to be in Heaven.

As the ceremony ended and the processional departed, I couldn't wait to get out of the church. At the age of 6 years 11 months, I was one of the taller kids in class, so I was close to the end of the procession. Now in my 60s, I'm only 5 feet 7, after shrinking 2 inches over time. When I think back on that day, it's ironic I was one of the "tall" kids. On that miserable day, I would have been happy to be a short guy and out the door quickly.

As I exited the pew, my eyes naturally went to the back of the church. I wanted to get through the maze of happy, smiling faces.

How dare they! Don't they realize what has happened?

I focused on a haggard, unkempt woman in a black raincoat, who looked vaguely familiar. It was Mom. Not the Mom I know. I had never seen her look this bad. Maturity has taught me the death of a loved one affects people differently, and Papa's death had caused grief that I had never witnessed. As I approached the rear of the church, Mom forced a smile, blew me a kiss and mouthed, "I love you."

The class had to go back to the school to be dismissed, and as I marched across the street, Mom was whisked away in a waiting car, back to the house. Later, when I walked out of school with my class, Dad and Uncle Don were waiting for me. The customary party following my First Communion was not going to happen.

Technically, Uncle Don wasn't related, but he was a very close family friend and my Godfather. He was there at my baptism and took his title and position to heart.

So Uncle Don took control of the situation that morning, and drove Dad and myself to the Lexington Dinner in Clifton, NJ. In those days, it was a dining car with maybe 12 to 15 spinning stools and 4 to 8 booths. We were men, so we sat at the counter. Uncle Don ordered sunny side eggs on a stack of pancakes. He told me this is the way I should eat them. It was ok, but I prefer them separate. For a little kid, breakfast with Dad and Uncle Don was huge.

You see, Uncle Don wanted to participate in my education. He wanted me to experience all that life had to offer. He made a fuss over my birthdays and special days. If he was busy, he had Aunt Rose (his wife) take me out. They both went overboard for me, especially considering they had seven children of their own. We went to places like Toots Shores, Radio City Music Hall, museums, The Bronx Zoo, West Point, etc. As a teen, Uncle Don went to a military prep school where he got the name "Moose." He taught me to box. I have a scar across the bridge of my nose, compliments of Uncle Don.

After my special breakfast, when we got back to the house, there were cars double parked, people on the sidewalk, front porch, stairway, and packed into the house. They kept coming and going, and I had to say hello and acknowledge all these people. Some I knew, some I didn't.

So much crying and hysteria. Grown men sobbing –strangers to me. Then somebody else walks in and it starts all over again. As each new arrival approached Mama, Mom, Aunt Marie, Uncle Ernie or Uncle Frank, the crying would continue and escalate to a higher pitch.

All of a sudden, Mama was on her feet, and was being helped with her coat. I asked, "Where are you going, Mama?" and she blurted out, "To see Papa."

Words which will remain with me forever.

ST Nicholas R.C. Church

Papa

In 1931, when Salvatore Marazano (leader of the Castellammarese clan and boss of bosses) was assassinated, his address book contained the address and phone number of Paul Palmeri.

In the wake of the The Apalachin Meeting the historic summit of the American Mafia that was held at the home of Castellammarese mobster Joseph "Joe the Barber" Barbara in Apalachin, New York on November 14, 1958.

The United States Senate Select Committee on Improper Activities in Labor and Management (also known as the McClellan Committee) was created by the United States Senate on January 30, 1957, and dissolved on March 31, 1960.

Robert Kennedy, Chief Counsel, for the committee, questioned John Charles Montana on July 2, 1958.

Mr. Montana had attended the Apalachin Conference and was probably the government's key to linking Organized 'Crimes strangle hold on labor and legitimate business

The following text of the hearing transcript establishes Paul Palmeri's prominence especially considering he died two and a half years earlier.

Castellamara Del Golfo Society Holds Banquet

The 25th anniversary banquet and ball of the Castellamara Del Golfo Society was held in Hotel Lafayette last night. Left to right: Paul Palmeri, toastmaster; John C. Montana, honor guest, and William L. Salacuse of Niagara Falls, honor guest.

Improper Activities In The Labor Field 12315

Mr. Kennedy. What about Paul Palmeri, of Buffalo?

Mr. Montana. I know who he is, because he had a brother in Buffalo, but I haven't seen him in 20 years.

Mr. Kennedy. Do you know of his criminal record?

Mr. Montana. I do not.

Mr. Kennedy. Here is a picture. Have you seen this picture of you and Mr. Palmeri, in 1939?

Mr. Montana. A picture of me?

Mr. Kennedy. Is this you?

The Chairman. I hand you a picture and ask you to examine it and state if you identify the persons on it. (Photograph handed to the witness.)

Mr. Montana. I think this picture was taken at the Rex Club in Niagara Falls and I was the speaker of the evening.

Mr. Kennedy. Who are the people?

Mr. Montana. Well, this is Palmeri here. The other man I don't remember. I don't know who he is.

Mr. Kennedy. Is that you and Paul Palmeri?

Mr. Montana. Well, that is one of them. There was other people at the speaker's table besides him. But he was the president of the Rex Club, which is the Republican Club in Niagara Falls.

Mr. Montana. I think this picture was taken at the Rex Club in Niagara Falls and I was the speaker of the evening.

Mr. Kennedy. Do you know of his criminal record.

Mr. Montana. I do not, sir.

Mr. Kennedy. And that some 15 years prior to this time he had been arrested about a dozen times?

Mr. Montana. I did not know about that.

Mr. Kennedy. From assault in the second degree to kidnaping? You did not know that at all?

Mr. Montana. I did not know it.

Mr. Kennedy. I don't believe this was the Republican Club. I believe it was a society meeting.

Mr. Montana. Well, I attend so many dinners, Mr. Kennedy, I

Mr. Kennedy. I believe it was a club meeting that had nothing to do with any political party. I have the name here.

Mr. Montana. Is it the Rex Club?

Mr. Kennedy. It is the Del Golfo Society.

Mr. Montana. That is their hometown society.

Mr. Kennedy. He had been arrested in Niagara Falls, Brooklyn, Chicago, New York, Springfield, Mass., Buffalo, and Lockport, N. Y.

Mr. Montana. I don't know anything about it.

Mr. Kennedy. Did you know that?

Mr. Montana. I do not, sir.

Mr. Kennedy. Did you know that he was held as a material witness in the Willie Moretti slaying?

Mr. Montana. I wouldn't know, sir.

Papa's Funeral

In 1955, Papa's death was a shock to the community, our family, and especially Mama. She was staying with us until after the funeral, something about not wanting to be in the home she shared with Papa. Besides, our house was the staging area for all of the out-of-state visitors. Lots of people to acknowledge and feed. Most of his friends and associates came under the cover of darkness, midnight till dawn. They wanted to pay their respects, but did not want to turn his wake and funeral into a circus or spectacle. Maintaining his anonymity.

The decision was made not to let the grandchildren attend the wake or the funeral. I guess between all the people in attendance and dealing with their own feelings, it was a good decision. Over the years, details of Papa's funeral were discussed by the family. While my memories and emotions are strong to this day, I was very young at the time. Most of what I know now, I learned later.

Papa had once intervened on behalf of a friend named Andrew Torregrossa, who owned funeral homes in Brooklyn. Turns out, Papa had represented at him at his "sit down," pleaded his case, and saved his life. Mr. Torregrossa was so grateful for Papa's help, he called Mama and implored her to be allowed to do Papa's funeral, no charge, to show his respect and gratitude.

As distraught as she was, Mama thanked him and explained that the boys (Ernie and Frank) were taking care of the arrangements. Ernie always said for the cost of the funeral, he could have buried Papa in a Cadillac.

Papa's wake was at Marrocco's Memorial Funeral Home in Passaic, NJ. It lasted 3 days. (Papa died on Saturday and was buried on Tuesday.) There was a High Mass at Our Lady of Mount Carmel Roman Catholic Church. A High Mass is when priests are in service instead of altar boys. The full church choir was also in attendance.

The funeral procession was led by 3 flower cars, several limousines, and endless cars. The cortage proceeded past Papa's home, which was customary, and then on to Calvary Cemetery in Paterson, NJ, where he was buried in a family plot. Papa's grave has an average headstone, with the name "Palmeri" inscribed on the face. The simple headstone was not typical for a man of power. As years went by, I spent lots of time at that gravesite, taking care of the plants for Mama, Aunt Marie and Mom.

Today, our family plot contains graves for Papa (1955), Nono (1961), Mama (1998), Mom (2000), Dad (2002), my sister Anne (2009) and Aunt Marie (2010).

The first grave in the family cemetery was my older brother, named Louis, who died at birth, in 1947. In 1959 (four years after Papa died), Aunt Marie's baby boy, also named Louis, was buried there a few days after he was born.

Mt Carmel R.C. Church

Before Papa Died

In the early 1950s, things were pretty good for our family. We lived in Passaic, NJ, at 84 Howe Avenue, on the second floor. Summers, Papa took us all to Atlantic City and the Hudson Valley. We stayed at a place called Canzoneris, an Italian resort in Newburgh, New York, owned by Tony Canzoneri, five time world boxing champion and Capo in the Bonanno Crime Family

Mom said when they rang the dinner bell I would go, "Num-num, num-num," which caused the other guests (adults) to follow suit chanting, "Num-num, num-num," which made Papa beam.

Most people are drawn to cute little kids, and if I say so myself, I was blonde, cute and advanced for my years, which I attribute to the time I spent with adults. My wife always says I didn't have a childhood, but that's not true. My childhood was split between cousins, a few carefully selected friends and school mates. But a lot of my growing up was influenced by the adults I was around.

The fact we lived in Passaic, closer to Mama and Papa than the rest of the family, put us in the forefront for their attention. We would see them on a daily basis, as opposed to the aunts, uncles, and cousins who would be at Sunday dinner once a week.

Christmas Eve With Santa

One of my earliest memories was when I was only 3 years old, and I was sick for Christmas. But even having a cold can't take away the anticipation of Santa's arrival. We could not go to Papa's for Christmas Eve dinner, so after dinner Papa, Mama and Aunt Marie came by our house to see me. After all, Christmas is for kids.

That night, I was charged up. Sure I was sick, but I was hyper and did not want to sleep because Santa was coming. Suddenly, the doorbell rang. Papa answered, and it was Santa Claus! Yes, Santa was at my door, wishing me a Merry Christmas.

Years later, I learned that when Papa offered "Santa" a drink and a tip, he declined both. But he said he may stop back after I was asleep. About an hour later, when I was in bed fighting my sleepiness, there was a knock on the door. There stood a distinguished man in a suit. He announced, "Merry Christmas, I am Santa Claus, and I would like that drink." He stayed for a while and disclosed that he was the president of a local bank, and on Christmas Eve he went door to door to excite the kids. I'm sure Papa's invitation and gesture intrigued him. I would bet no one else offered him a drink, let alone a tip.

Not So Cute

Even cute, kids will be kids. When I was 5, I had my tonsils out. I was staying at Papa & Mama's house, recuperating. I was a miserable, bored kid with a sore throat. At one point, when I couldn't find one of my toys, I looked for it under the fringed skirted couch. With a cigarette lighter, I set the couch on fire!!!

Dad, Aunt Marie and Papa were like the bucket brigade, putting out the flames. Tonsils or not, I was not in good graces that day.

I Heard There Was A Pot On

Papa used to spend a lot of time at our house. He regularly rang the bell at 10 or 11 at night, and when Mom buzzed him in, he would say he "heard there was a pot on," which meant he wanted her to cook macaroni, what else. If Mom didn't have sauce, she would make a marinara or *aglio et olio* (garlic and oil).

Always the curious kid, when people were in the house I wanted to see and hear what was going on. When Papa came by with his friends, if the talk didn't wake me up, the cooking smells did. If I could sneak a peek, I would see maybe four to six men at the table, all speaking Italian. The tone usually seemed serious, so I guess they were discussing business.

I was included in a lot, exposed to a lot, and learned a lot, but I was too young to be included in those dinner meetings. Later, I came to understand that our house was safe for Papa, not one of the normal places being watched.

Grooming

Papa and I were close and had a special relationship. I remember he would pick me up after school every Friday, and take me to the barber shop, where he would get a trim and manicure. Then I would get in the barber's chair. They would make noise with the scissors, and put tonic on, and comb my hair. Then to the manicurist table for a light file, soak, and buff.

I was definitely in Wise Guy training.

Papa was the epitome of a well-dressed, successful man. He wore impeccably tailored suits, with just the right break on his cuffs. He wore monogramed, perfectly starched white on white shirts, with cuffs that gave a peek at the daily selection of his diamond cufflinks, until he sat down and the full sparkle was unveiled. His ties were tied perfectly and screamed of power, long before anyone heard of the "power tie." He had a variety of rings and watches.

Even though I was only 5 or 6 years old, I knew I wanted to be as well dressed and groomed as Papa when I grew up.

Morales Bros. Bakery

Breaking Bread

On Sunday morning, Papa would take me to Mt. Carmel, his church. After mass, we would stop at Morales Bros Bakery and pick up two loaves of bread. It was my job to carry the bread.

Papa would pull his car in front of Morales Bros, like it was his own reserved parking space. People walking by acknowledged him like he owned the city. As we walked into the bakery, greetings were exaggerated, considering he was only picking up two loaves of bread.

As a young boy, I was impressed and proud to be with him. As an adult, my reflections tell me that people were hushed and respectful because of his power. While Papa always tried to stay low key, he was recognized in the community as a problem solver, a man of reason, and someone who could be relied on for counsel or help in an arbitration or family squabble.

As we rode back to his house, Papa would break off a piece of bread, and we ate it in the car. The fresh baked smell was enticing, and has stayed with me. A fond memory.

Tuesdays, Papa always picked up the special whole wheat bread, made only on Tuesdays at Morales Bros, and he dropped it off at our house for Mom. It was her favorite. When he would ring the bell, I ran downstairs to greet him, and retrieved Mom's bread.

The ritual of picking up fresh bread stayed with me into my adult years. I still get fresh baked bread and bring it home, only I have no one in the car to share it with.

Winky Dink

Papa would shave with a straight razor, while singing loudly to Italian opera records. During his dramatic ritual, I would sit close to the TV to listen to the muffled sound. One of my favorite TV shows was "Winky Dink and Friends."

I had a "Winky Dink" screen, which was a green plastic film you would place on the TV screen so you could draw pictures, play games and solve puzzles, along with the TV host, Jack Barry. Years later, Microsoft mogul Bill Gates praised this as "the first interactive TV show." The clever marketing scheme made the show understandable only if you purchased the special screen and crayons (for 50 cents).

One Saturday morning, while I was interacting with the TV host, Papa came out of the bathroom swinging the straight razor like a conductor's baton. When he saw me drawing on the TV screen, he screamed for Mama to stop me. "Elena! Elena!"

Papa was furious. But Mama calmed him down, and peeled the screen film corner to show him it was harmless. So he restarted the record and returned to singing and conducting.

Mom and Papa

Papa's Temper

A memory that has lingered, but I do not relish, was Papa's temper. For a man who was seemingly always in control, when he lost it, he was scary. You see, sometimes you have to get someone's attention to make sure your point is made.

This temper transferred and settled with Uncle Ernie, Dad and myself.

I hated to experience their wrath, whether directed toward me or others, so I was surprised that I inherited the trait. As dominant and borderline cruel to his children as Papa was, he always catered to Mom and me. Which raises the question, was he really loved? Or feared and respected? And could the people he touched with his powerful presence mask or suppress their feelings?

For example, when Mom was asked to a college prom, of course the young man asked Papa's permission. On the night of the prom, Mom came to dinner in a robe. Papa asked why she wasn't dressed for dinner. She told him it was the night of the prom. Papa said she wasn't going. He must have had a hair across his ass. Mom was devastated, but it shows the control he had to have. Personally I think it was sick and abusive.

Once when Uncle Ernie was in his 30's, he was in the middle of a card game and Papa walked in. Ernie acknowledged Papa and said, "I'll be with you in a minute, Papa." Ernie finished the hand and got up to kiss his father. Papa slapped him in front of all present. Papa said, "I'm your father. You will show me respect when I enter a room." Papa was a gambler and knew full well you don't get up from the table and leave your hand.

Uncle Frank said the real reason for the slap and comments was because Ernie had not been home in a couple of days. The irony is, after moving to Niagara Falls, Papa didn't come home and Mama went to Ziu Angelo (Papa's older brother and head of the family business). When Papa came home, he read Mama the riot act, "You never call my brother to look for me. When I come home, I come home."

Early in my marriage, I went out with the guys, got very drunk and went to sleep in the car. When I woke up, it was daylight. I was on my way home when I passed my brother, who was out looking for me. Sunday, we went to Mom's for dinner and my wife Sandi had attitude. Mama asked her what was wrong. Sandi started to spew. Mama told her the story about Papa, but I didn't get a pass.

Left to Right: Uncle Frank, Generoso Pope Publisher of IL Progresso Italian newspaper, and Uncle Ernie

Papa's Status & Influence

Papa was old school, especially in light of his age. He represented the family interests at most out of state meetings. He entertained out of state visitors, famous and infamous. Remember, Niagara Falls was a popular vacation spot and the number one honeymoon destination.

Papa had a guest list of prominent politicians and business men. Because of his communication skills, he was a close associate of Generoso Pope, the publisher of *Il Progresso*, the Italian language newspaper. And of course Papas main associations were with the who's who of the underworld.

Papa followed the old school manual and blueprint: be respectfully visible and conduct your business in private. He had his brushes with the law, but for the most part he was under the radar.

Papa and Mama were always active in the community politically and through church functions. They were highly regarded in these circles and being part of many beneficial projects bolstered Papa's image of respectability.

Often, Papa would take me with him as he went to meet with different people. Looking back, I see that my innocent presence was part of his cover, as always the doting Papa.

Although I was young, some things stick with me. I have a vague memory of Willie and Sally Moretti. We met with Albert Anastasia, Frank Costello, Anthony Bonasera, and Santo Volpe. I remember them distinctly, because they stayed in touch with Mama after Papa's death.

We met with others, whose names I don't remember readily. The meetings took place in luncheonettes, Italian delis, bakeries and coffee shops (people think Starbucks was innovative) and places I would later learn were "social clubs".

Mr. Pepetone

Another example of Papa's ability to blend was Mr. Pepetone, a non-assuming polite man, a widower with one adult daughter. Papa met him at one of the social clubs, took a liking to him and kind of brought him into his family. He would bring him to many different places and meetings like he did with me. He took him on the long drives, i.e. Pennsylvania, and they shared their love of opera, cuisine and Italian history. Mr. Pepetone was a civilian. After Papa died, Mr. Pepetone and his daughter would spend holidays with our family. He was genuinely liked and respected for being Papa's friend. As the years went by I met numerous Mr. Pepetone types, but they were far from being gentle. Most were stone cold killers. Lesson learned: "Don't Judge a Book by Its Cover".

GIFTS OF ITALY TO LIFE IN U. S. NOTED AT FETE

Speakers at Castellamare anniversary program cite notable contributions

Prominent Italian-Americans of the Niagara Frontier and other representative citizens last night praised the contribution of the Italian community to the city and country at the 25th anniversary banquet and ball of the Castellammare del Golfo Society in Hotel Lafayette.

The theme of remarks by younger guests, sons and daughters of those who immigrated from the Sicilian town from 1900 on, was expressed by President Andrew A. Abulone of the Young Castellammare Society, who stressed "our earnest desire and intent to carry on the torch you have borne so well for a quarter century."

Dr. Cono Ciufia, professor of surgery in Northwestern University and principal speaker, traced the history of the Sicilian community from pre-Roman times, urged appreciation of Italian cultural traditions and cited notable Italian-Americans and their contributions to the life of the nation.

Others who spoke were Rocco Spano, Italian consul; Peter Magaddino of Niagara Falls; Mary Cicina Gallo, medical technician at the General Hospital; John C. Montana, president of the Montedoro Society; Girolamo Turano, first president; Budget Director John J. Egan; Peter Fiorella, president of the Federation of Italian Societies, and Vincent Pierino, president of the society. Paul Palmeri was toastmaster. About 500 attended.

ITALIAN GIFTS TO U. S NOTED

Contributions of Italian-American citizens of Buffalo to city and country were cited last night by prominent Italian-Americans of the Niagara Frontier at the 25th anniversary banquet and ball of the Castellammare del Golfo Society in Hotel Lafayette.

Andrew A. Abulone of the Young Castellammare Society told older members of "our earnest desire and intent to carry on the torch you have borne so well for a quarter of a century."

Principal speaker was Dr. Cono Ciufia, professor of surgery at Northwestern University, who reviewed contributions to American life by notable Italian-Americans.

Other speakers included: Rocco Spano, Italian consul; Peter Magaddino of Niagara Falls; Mary Cicina Gallo, medical technician at General Hospital; John C. Montana, president of Montedoro Society; Girolamo Turano, first president; Budget Director John J. Eagan; Peter Fiorella, president of the Federation of Italian Societies, and Vincent Pierno, president of the society. Paul Palmeri was toastmaster.

Castellammare Society Marks Silver Jubilee

Shown at the 25th anniversary banquet and ball of the Castellammare del Golfo Society last night in Hotel Lafayette are, left to right, Dr. Cono Ciufia of Northwestern University, principal speaker; Cecina Gallo, technician at General Hospital, who also spoke; Paul Palmeri, toastmaster, and Stephen C. Magaldino, general chairman.

INDICTMENTS BARE HUGE BOOTLEG RING

Evasion of $3,429,500 Alcohol Taxes Laid to 69—Wealthy Land Owner Included

The smashing of a bootleg alcohol ring described by Treasury Department investigators as the biggest illicit liquor producing organization ever uncovered was announced here yesterday. The evasion of Federal taxes amounting to $3,429,500 was attributed to sixty-nine defendants named in an indictment obtained by Raymond Ickes, Assistant United States Attorney.

Besides six men described as bootleggers with careers originating in the days of prohibition, and a large number of others, the true bill named Simeon Brady, wealthy land owner and real estate operator of Somers, in Westchester County. Brady's son, Simeon Jr., also a defendant, was charged with having permitted other members of the ring to use a chicken coop on his farm at Towners, Putnam County, for the storage of sugar, urea and yeast, needed ingredients for alcohol production.

The elder Brady's part in the affair was said to involve the maintenance of a 1,000-gallon still on his farm. This plant, according to the Treasury men, was operated from October of 1937 to February, 1938. Taxes of $243,000 were alleged to have been evaded on the 121,000 gallons of alcohol, which, according to the government, was produced here.

Although the still on the Brady farm was described as a productive one, it was not nearly so successful, according to the charges, as another on the Fred Scoralick Farm, at Beekman, in Dutchess County. That one was said to have been kept going from November of 1934 to November of 1936, during which it turned out 366,000 gallons of spirits, on which taxes of $732,000 were alleged to have been evaded.

Other big plants listed were those in the Staples Brickyard, East Kingston, in which $630,000 taxes were evaded, and at the David Klinger Garage, 509 West Street. From July to October of 1939, it was charged, a 1,000-gallon still at the latter address turned out 190,000 gallons of spirits, on which the ring neglected to pay taxes of $427,500.

The investigation leading to the indictment was conducted by Thomas Buckley, Terry Rizza, Donald C. Young and Thomas Osborne of the Alcohol Tax Unit. All but four of the defendants are in custody.

The group described as principals of the ring were Vito (Brewster Bill) Giallo, and Paul Palmeri, both of Brewster, N. Y., and Giuseppe (Little Joe) Bosco, Tom (Big Tom) Calabia, Leo (Big Leo) Florino, and Nino Valenti, alias Jimmy Cupumano, all of New York City.

BOOTLEGGER TRIAL BEGINS

42 Men Accused of Defrauding U. S. of $3,500,000 Taxes

Forty-two men accused of having conspired in the operation of a bootleg alcohol industry said to have evaded Federal taxes of $3,500,000 between 1933 and 1941 were placed on trial yesterday in Federal court. The group was described by Edward Wallace, assistant United States attorney, as having operated nineteen stills in Dutchess, Westchester, Putnam, Ulster and Columbia Counties, and one in Manhattan.

Those on trial included the alleged leaders of the organization, Vito (Brewster Bill) Gallo, Paul Palmeri and Nini Valenti, all of Brewster, N. Y. A severance of trial was granted to Simeon Brady Jr. and his father of Somers, N. Y., who were described as financial backers of the alleged ring. The case against these two was set over to Feb. 1.

Palmeri and Others Arrested as Kidnapers Are Freed in Chicago

Callinan Says He Knows of No Grounds for Rumors of Chicago Gangsters Meeting and Plotting Abductions Here.

Five men, including Paul Palmeri, Falls undertaker, who have been held in Chicago as suspects in recent kidnapings, were released in Chicago yesterday, according to dispatches received from that city today. Coincidentally with the report of the release of the men, Chief of Detectives George H. Callinan yesterday disclaimed any knowledge of grounds for rumors that this city is the headquarters of the alleged kidnaping gang said to have been rounded up in Chicago.

According to the rumors circulated the alleged gang, reported to have been implicated in more than 100 kidnapings, often made this city its hideout. Chief Callinan also denied rumors that members of Al Capone's gang had held a confab here some months ago. He said that he never heard of any of Capone's gangsters ever having been in this city. The confab, according to police reports at the time, was said to have been of "Bugs" Moran gangsters instead of a Capone group.

Regarding the release of the suspects in Chicago the Associated Press carried the following dispatch from Chicago today:

"Chief of Detectives William Schoemaker said he had found no evidence to connect the men with the abduction of Alexander Berg of St. Louis and Ralph J. Pearce of Rockford, Ill.

"We are still investigating the matter and will keep these men under surveillance," Schoemaker said.

"Police authorities had previously asserted that the arrest of the five men had broken up a kidnaping syndicate which held more than 100 victims for ransom and collected hundreds of thousands of dollars in the last year.

"The other men arrested Monday and released today were Frank Chiavavoloti of Chicago, Paul Palmeri of Niagara Falls, N. Y., Angelo Caruso of New York, and Sylvester Agoglia of Chicago.

"Louis Spenilli, New York, who was quoted by police as admitting that he had acted as a go-between in the Berg kidnaping, was not released. He was arrested first and led police Monday to a street corner where he said he was to have met the kidnapers and paid them $100,000. Maggano and the four other men were found there in an automobile and arrested. They denied knowing anything about the kidnaping."

PAUL PALMERI ONE OF GANG SUSPECTED OF ABDUCTING BERG

Falls Undertaker Held with Capone Gangsters in Chicago; Hunt for Victim.

MAY BE ST. LOUIS MAN

Secrecy Shrouds Probe as Report Says Arrests Are Linked with Berg Case.

CHICAGO, Nov. 10.—Lawrence Mangano, leader of the west side Capone syndicate, and five other men were held at the detective bureau last night while authorities scoured the city in search for a kidnap victim the gang is reported to be holding for ransom.

While investigators maintained the utmost secrecy, the Herald and Examiner said it was reported that the victim was Alexander Berg, wealthy fur dealer of St. Louis, seized in that city Friday night.

The other five held are Louis Spenilli, Frank Chiavavollitti, Sylvester Agoglia, Angelo Caruso and Paul Palmeri. Caruso is of New York City, while Palmeri is a Niagara Falls, N. Y., undertaker.

No Police Record Here.

Chief of Detectives George H. Callinan of the Niagara Falls police department today said that Paul Palmeri under arrest in Chicago, has no police record here.

Six Held in St. Louis

ST. LOUIS, Nov. 10.—Five men and a woman were arrested and held today by police in connection with the kidnaping of Alexander Berg, wealthy fur executive who was abducted early last Friday evening and is still missing.

Police did not disclose their names, nor what evidence they have that those arrested may be connected with the kidnaping. They said one of them was the brother of a notorious former gang leader of St. Louis and the woman was the wife of a brother of another gangster.

The six were arrested in a raid on a house at Fern Glen, in St. Louis county, of William 'Bow Wow' McQuillan, who is at liberty under $15,000 bond, charged with violating the Harrison anti-narcotic act. McQuillan, however, is not one of those held, police said, nor was he at the place when the raid was made.

After Papa Died

After Papa died, Mama commenced my education. The pieces began to fit together for me in a way of amazement, honor and pride. Coupled with my ability to read the newspapers, I was enamored with Papa's position.

Prior to Papa's death, Mama always had praises for her beloved husband. After his death, even more so. While Mama always held Papa in high esteem in all her stories, it wasn't until I was a teen, and through my own research, that I realized how smart he really was.

Marocco's Funeral home

The Walk to Mama's

A week or two after Papa died, I went by myself to my church, St. Nicholas, where I also went to school. After church, I decided to walk to Mama's to visit her. That Sunday, Dad was out with the family car and Mom was stuck in the house with my kid sister and brother, Anne and Jody (Joe hates being called "Jody"). Believe it or not, in 1955, it was safe for a 7 year old to be out alone on a Sunday.

So, after church I walked to Morales Bros bakery, which is quite a few blocks from St. Nicholas. I picked up a loaf of bread, asked Mr. Morales to put it on Mr. Palmeri's account, and proceeded to walk to Mama's house. It was over a mile away.

When I left the bakery, I walked by Our Lady of Mt. Carmel, Mama and Papa's church. It was predominately Italian, founded in 1912 by Italian immigrants. Mt. Carmel was where Mom and Dad were married and where I was baptized. And later, where me and my cousin Big Paul were the altar boys at Aunt Marie and Uncle Ange's wedding.

As I continued, I was walking along the same route as Papa's funeral procession. I turned onto Passaic Street, which was lined with shops and stores of all kinds. In the '50s, there were stores that sold only men's hats, shoes, socks, ties, belts and underwear; and stores that sold ladies hats or ladies foundation garments; and stores that sold televisions and radios. Believe it or not, these businesses made an honest, respectable living. Sure, people were poor, but jobs were available, and unless you were disabled, nobody was looking for a handout. Compared to today, definitely a better time for most.

As I crossed Main Avenue, Passaic Street became Passaic Avenue. On my left, surrounded by a wrought iron fence, was a fountain, which was decorated at Christmas. It was the site for an interesting incident years prior, involving Uncle Ernie.

To the right was Marocco's Funeral Home, a big white mansion which was built by a wealthy industrialist and subsequently turned into a funeral home. Although I was too young to attend Papa's wake, Marocco's was a place where we spent a lot of time over the years. One of the leading pastimes for Italians are wakes and funerals.

When I returned from eight years living in Houston, Texas, I would get my morning call and updates of deaths and the arrangements

As I headed up Passaic Avenue, birds were chirping, cars cruising slowly, and people were walking to and from church. Quite the dichotomy of the climate on my First Communion day.

I finally arrived at Mama's house. Aunt Marie answered the door. She was my Godmother and special aunt, who always looked after me and was one of my biggest advocates. She lived with Papa and Mama for years, and didn't get married until later in life.

When Aunt Marie saw me, she asked, "Where is your mother?" and I said, "Home." She asked, "How did you get here?" I replied, "I walked."

Both Aunt Marie and Mama were happy to see me, but concerned that I walked the distance. The Palmeris were not very athletic. Anyway, that walk was talked about for years. You'd think I climbed Everest.

The Last Big Family Christmas

After Papa's death, individually everybody was ok, but without him to keep us all together and in line, things were different.

Eventually, Sunday dinners were not mandatory. Each family had their own Sunday dinner. We were still all together for holidays and special occasions, but that slowed over the years. A family that was once inseparable was hardly together a few years later. The main excuse was too many people, each family's commitments to in-laws, etc.

But in 1957, as a surprise for Mama, Uncle Ernie arranged for the cousins from Buffalo and their families to come to New Jersey for a traditional Christmas. In addition to the family and usual friends, there were new faces, including Angelo Petricca, who would two years later become Uncle Ange when he married Aunt Marie.

It was quite an event. On Christmas Eve, at six o'clock there was the traditional striped bass sautéed with shrimps and clams served over linguine. As a child I hated this dish, as a teen I acquired a taste for it, as an adult it is one of my favorites. Dinner was followed with fruit and pastries. There were presents for all. Then, at midnight, we could eat meat so we had sausage, Italian cold cuts, octopus, and more fruit and pastries.

The amazing thing, as years went on, there were "too many" of us to get together, but that year we were 40 to 45 people, in a 1500 square foot split-level house. We ate in shifts. Everybody had a good time and a lasting memory of how things use to be.

"Papa" & "Mama"

I don't recall the exact time and place, but if memory serves me, I was about 12 years old when I heard someone say something about "Papa". But I knew from the context they couldn't be talking about Papa. When I got home, I confided in my mother, as usual, and expressed my concerns for what I heard.

Mom told me the people were talking about *their* Papa.

What do you mean "their Papa?" I didn't get it. So she explained.

Until that moment, "Papa" & "Mama" were special names for my grandparents and for our exclusive use. I didn't realize there were other people called "Papa" or "Mama".

Growing up, I thought I knew a lot. And I did. I was educated, street smart and spent a lot of time with adults. But it just goes to show what a sheltered life I led.

Mama And Papa

Mama Said

Mama said, "Lou Lou, you should be a pharmacist."

Mama

Mama (Elena Curti Palmeri) was 58 when Papa died, and she followed the customary seven years of mourning. She wore black and had masses said for him, which we all attended.

When asked about the possibility of dating or having a male companion, she emphatically proclaimed, "I was married to the best! I had a wonderful life!" She also would say, "Who or what could ever be deserving of my attention?" Papa may have been powerful, but Mama was special too. And she knew it.

These days you here the phrase "70 is the new 60" or "60 is the new 50," etc., because a large segment of today's population is more active and youth oriented. Mama was youthful and beautiful for any age and in all decades. She was contrary to the matronly dress and makeup for mothers and grandmothers of the 1950's and the old lady look in the Italian community (stereotypically dark dress to the floor, gray hair pulled into a bun, dark stockings and no makeup.) After the 7 year mourning period, and until she was 95, Mama would only be seen in silk dresses hemmed to just cover her knee, with fashionable pumps. She had perfectly coiffed hair, with no gray ever. She was meticulously manicured and pedicured.

Mama was about five feet tall and full figured, as they say. She was not physically active. The world had not heard of jogging or aerobics. She had domestic help, and until the early 1950's her mother (who we called "Nono") did all the cooking. Mama's porcelain skin and regal stature made her stand out in all venues. When she was with Mom and/or Aunt Marie, people assumed they were sisters. When I was with her from the age of 5 till my 40's, people assumed she was my mother.

Mama was blessed with wonderful genes. Nono died at 99 (one month shy of 100.) Mama's sister, Aunt Blanche (Bianca) died at 100. And their father died at 83.

On the other hand, Papa's family tended to die young, suddenly, from bad health. Uncle Angelo died from a stroke at 54, Papa from a heart attack at 62. No, my relatives were not "whacked" — if that's what you're expecting.

Mama's Stories

Growing up, I had a close relationship with both Mama and Papa. But with Papa gone, I knew Mama needed people around to help her transition into her new life. As I started spending more time with her, she began telling me our family history. Some days, I would walk to Wasser's Luncheonette on Broadway in Passaic where Mama would meet Aunt Marie almost daily for lunch.

From the time I spent with Papa, I knew he was different than other men. My father, uncles, and their friends and associates were different from all the other men I encountered: priests, bakers, milkmen, repairmen, my friends' fathers, etc. When Mama began telling me her stories about the family, she delivered them in a way as to be revered, as did all the other adults. My family is proud of their claim to fame in Italian American history. The stories, commentary and interactions with Papa's friends and admirers had a profound impact on me. Then and now.

Early on, I copped an attitude that we were different from the average person. The truth is, with Papa dead, we were pretty much average. Some kids aspire to be baseball, football, basketball stars, rock stars and Academy Award winners. I did too. But my true and lasting aspiration was to take my rightful place as a high-ranking mobster.

Over the years, despite all the changes, zero loyalty, RICO investigations, etc., I never lost the desire, the imagery, the exposure to The Life. Even knowing full well that danger was ever-present. When given the opportunity to flex my muscle or to prove my balls were made of cast iron, I rose to the occasion. Don't let anyone bullshit you. When you're in a tough situation, the adrenalin starts, you just keep telling yourself, "no matter what happens, show them you're all man."

I often say I was a great student. But it's more a result of the image than the reality.

Breakfast with Mama

After Papa died, I started spending just about every Friday night with Mama and Aunt Marie. On Saturday mornings, Mama would make breakfast. Usually oatmeal. She always had Quaker Oats, the kind you cook, not instant. Sometimes she had Nabisco shredded wheat, a favorite from Niagara Falls, where Nabisco had a massive plant that employed hundreds of people. Shredded wheat was served to tourists after riding the Maid of the Mist, the boat ride in the Niagara River. Those were the days when major corporations made a profit on the hard work of United States citizens, the days before corporate America outsourced us into welfare, food stamps and subsides too numerous to list, turning the tables and industrializing third world countries, while embarking us to the brink of being third world ourselves.

Mama always had a small bowl of stewed, pitted prunes. We would have a small glass of orange juice, oatmeal or shredded wheat, sometimes with fruit. She would place two cups on the table, one was filled with milk and the other was empty. She would pour herself a cup of coffee. Then she would pour a drop of coffee into my cup. She only drank Martinson coffee, which came in a red and gold can. Also on the table was Savoiardi (Italian lady fingers) that came from Deana's pastry shop on Passaic Street in Garfield, NJ.

Mama would sit facing the picture window that exposed two massive oak trees as we ate and talked. She loved to watch the squirrels dart up and down the trees. With the sidelight windows open slightly, we could listen to the birds chirp. Mama always broke a piece of bread or cookie and threw it in two different directions, one for the squirrels, the other for the birds. We were always told not to feed the squirrels and birds, but we never listened to authority; we did what we thought was right.

As she settled in, sometimes Mama would talk about all the travel, banquets, weddings and galas they attended in all the cities where Papa had friends and associates. Not just New Jersey, but everywhere, from the central US, to the East Coast, North to South. Her favorite places were Saratoga Springs, NY and Hot Springs, Arkansas. Along with Chicago, Detroit, Cleveland, Miami, and, of course New York City.

Mama was one of the few wives that traveled with their husbands for business. Sounds like a loving thoughtful gesture, but bringing Mama helped Papa's anonymity and his professional image. (Pretty slick.)

Mama would radiate when she spoke of the reception Papa would receive. It was honor, respect, and genuine love. She would glow when she described the standard greeting Papa received, "Bono Sera, Don Palo" or "Paolino." And of course she was "Signora." After the official greetings, they were just "Paul and Elena." When they attended a political affair or any civilian gathering, the greetings were not as elaborate, but they were warm and respectful for Paul and Helen.

Mama told stories of Papa's business and associates in a tone that would make anyone want to be in The Life, let alone an impressionable seven year-old.

Goodfella

The first time I heard the term "GOODFELLA" was from Mama. We were having breakfast and she referred to someone, and said he was a "Good Fella." Although her command of the English language was masterful, every now and then she would say something I thought was off. (She always referred to macaroni as "macaronis"). It wasn't until years later that I realized the significance of her use of "GOODFELLA".

Mama Said be a Pharmacist

After breakfast, I would watch my favorite TV shows: Saturday morning westerns like Roy Rogers and Dale Evans, The Cisco Kid, Hopalong Cassidy, The Lone Ranger, Rin Tin Tin, Sargent Preston of the Yukon, and Sky King. And don't forget the un-western "Winky Dink."

After my shows, we would go downtown to Marcus Drugs. When we walked in, we were greeted by clerks on the floor and behind the counters as we zig-zagged through and around point-of-purchase displays. The displays had everything from vitamins to makeup, face cream, and boxed candy. The store was devoted to these and all kinds of items.

We would sit at the lunch counter, just beyond the cash register and newspapers and magazines. Mama would order a cheeseburger and cherry Coke for me and a grilled cheese and cup of Salada tea for herself.

Mama was conflicted about my future. She would glorify "THE LIFE" but would always encourage me to be a "WHITE COLLAR MAN".

Her conversation was 180 degrees from breakfast. At the pharmacy lunch, she totally disregarded the benediction of The Life, and diligently explained the fruits of being a pharmacist.

Mama said, "Look, Lou Lou, the pharmacist!"

Mama said, "He wears a nice white coat. He is admired by all. He works in air conditioning." Remember, it was the 50's, and only bars, movies and pharmacies were air conditioned.

Mama said, "The pharmacist is respected like a doctor and doesn't work nights. He sells drugs, candy, makeup, and home health supplies. He sells newspapers, magazines, greeting cards. He has the breakfasts and lunches."

And her favorite: "He sells those little alarm clocks!" Baby Bens, she had one.

Papa & Mama's Early Years

As the story goes, Mama and Papa met across the soda fountain at Aunt Blanche's (Mama's sister) husband's confectionary shop, where Mama worked. Papa walked into store as Mama was tidying up. Their eyes met. They smiled. Mama was coy. They spoke briefly. Later, Mama told me about it, warm with memories.

"Papa was well dressed, charming. He had an air of confidence and stood so erect and tall. He invited me to accompany him to the theater. Of course, I told him I would have to ask my mother and father's permission. So they gave me permission. And we were married three months later."

"We settled in a flat on Houston Street in New York. Your mother Anne was born, my next baby died, and then Ernie." As time went on, Mama explained everything to me.

"Papa had to be able to move around in and out of the city. He was doing well, we were happy. Then Ziu Angelo sent Papa a message, that he wanted him in Niagara Falls. Ziu Angelo was the first boss of Buffalo and Niagara Falls." That's what Mama said, and it's true.

Buffalo Bill

P apa's older brother was Benedetto Angelo Palmeri, A/K/A Buffalo Bill, a name rumored to have been given to him because he wore a ten gallon hat and walked around with an exposed firearm and bodyguards. I believe the name came from a combination of his residency in Buffalo, along with his attire and swagger. He was "Ziu Angelo" or "Uncle Angelo" to our family, but it was with fervent respect when one of the elders referred to him as "Buffalo Bill".

He was "Don Nitto" to the Italian citizens, who he helped when their pride kept them from seeking welfare. He was a one man welfare agency. I like to think of him as an Italian Robin Hood. While he was responsible for feeding, clothing and heating the homes of many, he made his money in numerous illicit activities.

Buffalo Bill had all the standards: gambling, prostitution, protection, loan sharking, and because of his location, a lucrative white slavery and narcotics trade. Contrary to all the disclaimers from Carlo Gambino, Joe Bonanno, Paul Castellano, et al, dope was one of their original and perennial money makers.

When The Volstead Act (Prohibition) passed in 1919, Angelo Palmeri had the infrastructure and everything in place to control the flow of liquor from Canada. Historians are conflicted when declaring the first boss of Buffalo. I can assure you that Buffalo Bill was the first and only boss in Buffalo and Niagara Falls until his death on December 21, 1932.

Apparently historians, and for that matter most Mafia Families from the 1950s forward, do not subscribe to the model where the boss is in the background and the street boss gets all the glory and the heat. Ironically, the Genovese family eventually did adopt a street boss model and in the 1960s went to a three man ruling panel model.

I find it amusing, when I read the accounts as reported by people who have basically reiterated others' writings, especially if you believe the adage "If you tell a story enough times it must be true." I wasn't there, but based on all I was told from the age of five by all the adults in my life, I stand firm on my assertions. I'm sure that every family member, individually, did not decide to make up a story for an impressionable kid.

Buffalo Bill was a Character

Uncle Angelo transported his own wine when visiting Canada. Pretty interesting, considering he controlled the flow of illegal liquor from Canada.

Mama told me about the time Buffalo Bill was trying to avoid arrest. He was hiding in a friend's home, in a second floor bedroom, all dressed up, when he was arrested and charged with murder.

Angelo Palmeri, like his brother Paul, loved opera and to sing arias. Singing was a trait that passed down to Uncle Ernie, myself, and some of the cousins. Obviously, for our own enjoyment. While being held without bail, Buffalo Bill brought his singing talent to a new and unlikely venue, the jail, entertaining his fellow prisoners and effectively pissing off the jailers.

The victim's wife, the key and only witness to the murder, went to New York for her husband's funeral. After that, she could not be located to testify. Buffalo Bill was released.

Mama said, "Ziu Angelo was a mad man behind the wheel. It was a terrible day for all of us when he died." He died in his car, but it wasn't a traffic accident. He was sitting behind the wheel of his automobile in his driveway when he suffered a massive stroke.

A WISER GUY

It was ironic that Buffalo Bill died in his car. He loved his car, although he was a terrible driver.

On top of that, he was so arrogant. At railroad tracks, he would blow his horn for the trains to stop for him so he could come through.

One afternoon, he lost control of his automobile and veered off the road, crashing through the storefront of a fish market. As the irate fish monger wove through the dust and debris, he quickly reversed field when he realized who was behind the wheel, and wittingly approached a disoriented Buffalo Bill, asking, "What can I get for you today, Mr. Palmeri?"

Sicilians are naturally superstitious. After Buffalo Bill died, a friend of Papa's told him about a man who was saying unflattering things and wishing him harm. The man who spoke those words was found hanging on a meat hook with his eyelids and mouth sewn shut. He would no longer be able to witness or say anything about anybody ever.

IS FINED $250.

Judge Brennan in city court today imposed a fine of $250 on Angelo Palmiera, convicted on a charge of assault, third degree. The Italian was arrested by Patrolman McNamara of the Franklin street station after it was alleged he drew a revolver and fired at the policeman. Antonio Sacca and Charles Valarosa, arrested on the same charge, were discharged. The testimony showed that the last two men did not interfere with the policeman when he was making an arrest.

GIVEN MAXIMUM SENTENCE FOR ATTACKING POLICEMAN

Angelo Palmieri of 68 Dante place was fined $250 by Judge William P. Brennan in City court for assaulting Patrolman Edward McNamara while the officer was making an arrest. The fine is the maximum fixed by law for simple assault. Antonio Sacca and Charles Valaroso, who were implicated in the fight in Dante place in which McNamara was assaulted, were discharged, as the police could not show that they engaged in the beating of the patrolman. The fight occurred a week ago.

SUSPECT ARRESTED IN CONNECTION WITH KILLING OF EMILO GNAZZIO SAID TO HAVE DRAWN MONEY AND PLANNED GETAWAY

Clever Work of Callinan, Senior Detective of Bureau and Prompt Cooperation of His Aides Effected Capture of Angelo Palmieri Without Firing of Single Shot— Prisoner Declines to Talk.

Angelo Palmieri, 43 years old, of No. 558 Portage road, is held by the Falls police in connection with the murder of Emile C. Gnazzio who was shot to death in front of No. 121 Eleventh street, on Monday noon. A charge of murder has been placed opposite Palmieri's name on the police blotter but he has not been formally arraigned in police court. He will be arraigned tomorrow, police said today. He was arrested late yesterday afternoon at the home of Samuel Rangatore, No. 420 Eighth street.

The police are seeking a second man in connection with the shooting. He is said to be a chauffeur who accompanied Palmieri on the day the shooting occurred. His identity is known and it is expected that he will be arrested within a few hours.

Palmieri, according to the police version of the shooting, is the man to whom Gnazzio owed money and to whom the murdered man refused to pay $5 interest on the loan. His occupation is given in the city directory as merchant. He is said to be wealthy and his wife and several children live at the Portage road address. He came here three years ago from Buffalo. He has been sought by the police since a short time after the murder. Since the search first started Palmieri has not visited his home, police say.

The capture of the suspect was featured by many dramatic incidents. His hiding place was revealed by careful investigation on the part of Detective George H. Callinan and his arrest followed the surrounding of the house in which he was hiding by detectives. Detectives Terrence M. Reilly, James Keenan and John L. Roeder aided Detective Callinan in the arrest of Palmieri.

Identity Known

The identity of the man alleged to have been implicated in the murder was known to the police late in the afternoon of the day the shooting occurred. Palmieri, the man they sought, is known to his intimates and the police as "Buffalo Bill." Realizing that Palmieri must have deposits of money in Falls banks and that he would need money if he wished to make a getaway, Detective Callinan set out to locate these accounts. He succeeded and he instructed officials of the bank to notify him immediately if any check came from Palmieri to be cashed. Yesterday morning he was notified that a check for $1,400 had been presented. This was the detective's cue and he set out to learn who had presented the check and ascertain, if possible, the hiding place of the man he sought. After an investigation he determined that Palmiere was in hiding in the Eighth street house.

Around 4 o'clock yesterday afternoon Callinan strolled leisurely up Eighth street and stopped at a house near the home where Palmieri was believed to be in hiding. He rang the doorbell of the neighbor's house and the woman of the house came in response to the ring. She looked mildly surprised when she saw Callinan in the door way but immediately asked him in.

The detective questioned her adroitly about doings in the house nearby.

"I am Detective Callinan," he told her, laughingly.

Sings Grand Opera

The police did not attempt to get any statement from Palmieri last night. No one was allowed to see him. Today he was brought into court before Judge Piper but no formal charge was placed against him. His case was put over until tomorrow and he was returned to his cell. He spent the morning singing loudly, mostly operatic airs.

Callinan said today that he had learned that the stage was all set for Palmieri's flight last night, and that the money drawn was to be used for this purpose. An automobile had been hovering about the house for several hours yesterday afternoon, the police were informed, but no attempt was made by Palmieri to leave the place, the desired opportunity not presenting itself.

"Yes I know, I've read about you," the woman replied.

Gnazzio Was Shot Over Money Dispute, Police Say; May Arrest Slayer Soon

Surrounding the Career of Murdered Man and His Wife Is a Romance That Reaches Through Several States, Neighbors Say.

That Emilo C. Gnazzio was shot to death because he would not pay $5 a month interest on a loan of less than $500 that had been made to him was the conclusion arrived at by Falls police today after several hours of investigation of the circumstances that surround the murder of the New York man in front of No. 121 Eleventh street, yesterday noon.

The police say they know the identity of Gnazzio's slayer and predict that he will be in custody within a few hours.

The theory that Gnazzio was slain by a jealous rival for a woman's affection, was entirely discarded by the police late yesterday. The woman with whom he lived at No. 123 Eleventh street, was his real wife, the police say. She was released by the police last night after she had made a statement regarding the trouble over money affairs which she asserts resulted in her husband's murder.

Gnazzio is said to have borrowed the money on a ring and pin. Yesterday he met the man who had advanced him the money and the latter demanded payment of the loan. Gnazzio is reported to have told him that he did not have the money and that he would pay it soon. He remarked that the money lended need not worry because he had the pin and ring as security. Then the demand for the $5 interest was made. An argument followed. The two separated but later the money lender, it is claimed by the police, returned and shot Gnazzio.

The body of the murdered man was turned over to Mrs. Gnazzio last night by Coroner W. L. Draper. It was taken to New York today for burial.

The result of careful inquiry among the residents of Eleventh street where Gnazzio lived is the story that the victim of yesterday's tragedy on the east side had been acquainted with his wife from early childhood. The two were raised in the same section in New York city. The woman is of American extraction. When the girl was sixteen she was induced by Gnazzio, it is told, to accompany him to Virginia, later migrating eastward to a point near their former home. In 1918 Gnazzio joined the U. S. navy and made an allotment from his service pay over to his wife who worked in department stores. On the man's discharge from the navy he failed to find steady work and came to this city. Subsequently his wife was induced to come here after storing their furniture. The woman is reported to have told her friends in the district that she was married in 1920. It was last April when the woman arrived in this city to join her husband. She was given charge of a little cigar store but a change in conditions in the district failed to insure wealth from the denizens of that section. Gnazzio is said to have been an inveterate gambler and a regular loser. He is also said to have been too free with his hands when prompted to slap the faces of those he believed he could handle. That he incurred the displeasure of many of his people is common report. Among the residents of Eleventh street revenge because of his pompous demeanor and irritable ways, may have prompted the act. It is also told that Gnazzio, becoming short of funds, permitted his wife to be out of his sight more frequently than he used to.

The removal of Gnazzio, who is said to be known in New York at times under the name of Ferisa, a family name, may, it is told, signal the recall of the widow to her own people.

PALMERI FUNERAL SERVICES SATURDAY

Reputed Gang Leader Never Convicted of Crime

Angelo (Buffalo Bill) Palmeri, 52, once a power in the underworld, will be buried Saturday in Pine Hill cemetery following funeral services at the home at 295 Jersey street. The hour for the funeral had not been set today.

Palmeri died yesterday afternoon at the wheel of his auto in the driveway of his home. A stroke of apoplexy was blamed.

Although Palmeri 10 years ago was reputed to be the head of a blackhand extortion gang, police never succeeded in pinning a crime on him. He was fined $250 once on an assault charge, and questioned numerous times about other offenses, but his only time behind bars was spent there as a witness.

He and the father of Joseph Di Carlo, recently branded by Police Commissioner Roche as Public Enemy No. 1, were closely associated before the elder Di Carlo's death.

Their methods of operation were different, police said, Di Carlo being a smooth, peaceful worker and Palmeri more inclined to violence, but they provided mutual protection for each other.

In 1924 Palmeri was arrested with Joseph Di Carlo for questioning in the shooting of Joe Pattitucci, government witness in a narcotic case involving Di Carlo.

Pattitucci lived to testify against Di Carlo, resulting in the latter being sentenced for interferring with a government witness. The narcotic case was dropped, and Palmeri was freed.

Palmeri was born in Castellammare, Sicily. He came to this country in 1906 and to Buffalo in 1912. A wife and four daughters survive him.

Record Funeral Is Expected As Hundreds Mourn Palmeri

Known to Police as "Buffalo Bill," West Side Figure Was Benefactor of Italian Colony.

While the passing of Angelo B. Palmeri was noted without regret by the police, his death Wednesday brought sincere expressions of sorrow from hundreds of American citizens of Italian ancestry whom he had befriended in times of need.

And it seemed certain Thursday that when the funeral services are held Saturday morning, his former home, 295 Jersey street, and Holy Angels church in Porter avenue, would be crowded with a host of mourners—that the funeral procession would be the largest ever turned out for an Italian-American citizen of Buffalo.

Chief mourners are the widow, Mrs. Laura Palmeri, and her four children, Sarah, 17; Anna, 12; Gloria, 9, and Rose, 8, but many tears will be shed by that host of others whose homes were heated, whose tables were made bountiful, whose children had been clothed out of the largess of Angelo B. Palmeri.

Wore Five-Gallon Hat.

To the police he was known as "Buffalo Bill," because he affected five-gallon hats and carried a pistol in a holster in full view of any who cared to look, but to the citizens of the lower West side he was "Don Nitto"—a term connoting respect and affection.

To the police he was known as the man they arrested in 1915 on an assault charge, the man who paid $250 after his conviction—but to the citizens of the lower West side he was the smiling, singing "Don Nitto" who passed out $5 and $10 bills to tide his lowly friends over until work became more plentiful.

To the police he was known as a man who had close contact with many illicit enterprises, who had such power that he was able to bring peace between warring liquor runners—but to the citizens of the lower West side he was their individual welfare department, a man who could and would aid them when pride kept them from appealing to the organized charities.

Born in Sicily.

"Well, that's one more man we won't have to watch," a police official said.

"Last night he gave me help and tonight he told me to return for more," a Busti avenue resident said, tears filling his eyes, when he learned Wednesday that he would have to cancel the engagement and to struggle along without the help of "Don Nitto."

Palmeri was born in Castellamare, Sicily, 52 years ago. He came to this country in 1906.

His first job in New York was as a dock laborer. In 1912 he came to Buffalo and opened a saloon in 99 Dante place.

A wave of sadness swept through the lower West side when it was learned Palmeri had died of a heart attack while seated in his automobile in front of his home Wednesday afternoon.

Especially sad were the members of upwards of a score of families whose only source of food each Christmas for years had been Angelo B. Palmeri.

Papa was a Gambler

Papa was a serious gambler. One time, after he had been gone for days, he came home and passed out on the bathroom floor, next to an open empty suitcase. When he had left home a few days before, the suitcase was filled with cash.

Mom was a little girl when she stumbled upon this scene. She called out, "Mama, Papa is sleeping on the floor." So Mama proceeded to walk her daughter out of the bathroom. Then she got a cold washcloth and attended to Papa.

Papa & The Funeral Home

Alfred Panepinto had no luck at all. He lost his funeral home business to Papa in a card game. Then, years later, Panepinto was shot dead in a card game.

While proliferating his image as a respected funeral director, Papa was recognized as a leader in the Italian community. He was a sought- after orator, president of the Rex club (the Republican club) and he hosted a radio show.

After winning the funeral home, Papa wanted to secure his position, so he told Uncle Ernie to go to school for a license. Ernie refused, causing battles between father and son. (Honor thy father.) My mother could not stand the fighting, so she stepped in the middle. She offered to go to school and get the funeral director's license. It wasn't the first time she covered for Ernie.

Mama Heard:
St. Valentine's Day Massacre

When business associates met with Papa at their house, Mama used to stand outside the French doors to his office and listen. No wonder she knew so much about what was going on.

The one story from Mama's collection that established the importance and prestige of the Palmeri family and set the tone for my interest, attitude and pride, were events leading up to the St. Valentine's Day Massacre. That infamous event in Chicago was such a shocking display of violence that even little kids knew of it, kinda like Adolph Hitler. There are some things that the masses are more aware of than others.

Papa always had out of town visitors and guests. One time, while two of these guests were visiting, and Mama was doing her usual reconnaissance, she heard them discussing with Papa about a job in Chicago.

Some of what was written about the St. Valentine's Day Massacre states that Al Capone requested "out of town Sicilians" for the job. Mama knew most of the details and the Sicilians' assignment. And when the news broke, she put the pieces together. Bear in mind the title, St. Valentine's Day Massacre, was coined after the event.

Papa's Friends

Mama always talked about Papa's friends. Albert Anastasia, Santo Volpe, Tony Bonasera — these were men I saw on a regular basis. I knew they were close to Papa, but never realized the bond until years later.

Some guys just don't get it. Following the violence of 1930-31, they abandoned the "Boss of Bosses" title and went to a Board of Directors model called "The Commission," whose main function was to keep things peaceful and orderly. Without war, everybody spends time earning, which is more beneficial for all. One guy that didn't get the message was John Bazzano, the Pittsburgh Boss who killed the Volpe brothers (no relation to Santo) without permission, in an attempt to eliminate Neapolitans. This was at least one time these men pooled their collective talents. I'm sure there were others. Bazzano was then summoned to a dinner meeting in New York to answer for his actions, where he got the surprise dessert.

Mama also talked about Russell Bufalino and Joe Barbara (the Apalachian Meeting host). Both of them got their start with Buffalo Bill. As did Willie Moretti.

In the late 1920s, the New York City guys wanted Papa to come back, but he was happy in the Falls out of the line of fire.

From there, he could go anywhere. So Papa told them to take his close associate and friend Willie Moretti, who proved he was more than capable.

Dr. Mario (DR. TAG) Tagliagambe son of Silvio Tagliagambe member of the D'Aquila (Gambino) Family

Murder Ring Suspects

Sam Di Carlo — Peter Lombardi — Michael Russo — Tony Bonasero
Robert Anastasio — John Addo — Angelo Colizza — Paul Palmieri

EIGHT OF SUSPECTS TAKEN IN ROUNDUP

COPS ROUND UP 14 AND SAVE BIG SHOT

Gangland's flare for staging wine and women orgies as a prelude to bloodshed, saved the life of a big shot Manhattan racketeer and caused the roundup of fourteen men suspected as members of a national murder ring, police announced yesterday.

Most of the prisoners — all paid executioners, according to detectives — were surprised in Manhattan and Brooklyn hotels as they

The late John Bazzano

were waiting to attend a party in a leading hostelry last night at which the death of their prospective victim would be celebrated in advance.

Killers to get $20,000.

At the height of the festivities, after the cooch dancers had done their turn and the liquor was producing vainglorious boasting, four of the merrymakers were to be handed $5,000 each for their last job, that of rubbing out John Bazzano, Pittsburgh racket czar, in Brooklyn Aug. 8, police said. The specific charge against the fourteen is the murder of Bazzano, who was stabbed—apparently with ice picks—and dumped into a sack in the middle of the highway at Centre between Clinton and Henry Sts., Brooklyn. Bazzano's body

cerned in either the grocery or restaurant business, were listed as follows:

Robert Anastasio, who spent eighteen months in the Sing Sing death house awaiting execution for murder several years ago; John Addo, alias Johnny Bath Beach of 1955 W. 10th St., Brooklyn, often in trouble with police; Tony Bonasero, alias the Chief, of 7515 13th Ave., Brooklyn; Ciro Gallo, of 708 Bushwick Ave., Brooklyn; Joseph Trainia, of 1778 71st St., Brooklyn.

Santo Volpe of Pittston, Pa., a relative of the slain Volpe brothers; Paul Palmieri of Niagara Falls, N. Y.; Angelo Colizza of Dunmore, Pa.; Sam Di Carlo of Buffalo, N. Y.; Carlo Sparling of Pittsburgh; Frank Adrana of Pittsburgh; Michael Bua of Pittsburgh; Peter Lombardi of Trenton, and Michael Russo of Pittsburgh.

Russo was said to be the only man armed when he was captured. An additional charge of Sullivan law violation was made against him.

At the arraignment, Samuel Leibowitz, counsel for the prisoners, declared, there was "not a scrap of evidence on which to hold them."

ARREST OF 14 FOILS MURDER FETE PLAN

Police Say Prisoners Intended to Toast Killing of Pittsburgh Man in Brooklyn Aug. 7

AND TO PAY OFF SLAYERS

New York Racketeer Reported Marked—Nine of Captives Are From Out of Town.

Instead of celebrating the murder of John Bazzano of Pittsburgh last night at a dinner in a midtown hotel as they had intended to do, according to the police, fourteen men rounded up in the city before dawn yesterday were held in Raymond Street jail in Brooklyn, accused of the murder.

Bazzano, described by the police as a Pittsburgh restaurant owner, was garroted, stabbed twenty-two times in the chest with an ice pick, tied in a sack and dumped in Centre Street, between Hicks and Clinton Streets, Brooklyn, the night of Aug. 7. He had been in this city four days.

Casting about for a motive for the murder, the police finally decided that it was probably done in retaliation for the killing of the Volpe brothers of Pittsburgh — James, Arthur and John—in Bazzano's coffee shop the night of July 29. The Volpes were alleged to be bootleggers.

Eight Out-of-Town Prisoners.

Four of the fourteen men held for the murder are from Pittsburgh and five are from the Bath Beach district of Brooklyn, the old stamping ground of the late Frankie Uale, yeoman of the guard for Al Capone. Most of the others are from Buffalo and vicinity.

The fourteen prisoners are: Michael Russo, 1,202 Fifth Avenue, Pittsburgh; Frank Adrana, 90 Washington Street, Pittsburgh; Michael Bua, 208 South Atlantic Street, Pittsburgh; Carlo Sparlino, 1,215 Pennsylvania Avenue, Pittsburgh; Santo Volpe, 215 Wyoming Avenue, Pittstown, Pa.; Angelo Calizza, Dunmore, Pa.

Also John Addo, alias Johnny Bathbeach, 1,965 West Tenth Street, Brooklyn; Ciro Gallo, 706 Bushwick Avenue, Brooklyn; Tony Bonasera, The Chief, of 7,515 Thirteenth Avenue, Brooklyn; Joseph Trainla, 1,778 Seventy-first Street, Brooklyn; Paul Palmieri, 1,535 Whitney Avenue, Niagara Falls, N. Y.; Sam Di Carlo, 274 Prospect Avenue, Buffalo, N. Y.; Peter Lombardi, 103 Greenwood Avenue, Trenton. N. J.; Robert Anastascio, 151 Sackett Street, Brooklyn.

Anastascio served fourteen months in the death house of Sing Sing Prison nine years ago for the murder of George Purello in Brooklyn, got out on appeal and was released after a second trial. He was a friend of Joe Farino, Brooklyn dock loader, who was arrested in his home borough in March, 1930, for the murder of "The Clutching Hand."

"The Clutching Hand" was Giuseppe Piraino, a Capone vassal. Both he and his son and at least five of their friends vanished from Brooklyn racketeerdom in 1930 through the zealous application of dagger and shotgun by a competing alcohol ring in the borough.

Lay Killing to Revenge.

Bazzano, the police believe, was lured to Brooklyn by some of his countrymen, soon after the murder of the Volpes, by the promise of some new source of revenue, though their real motive was to take vengeance on him for an alleged "double cross" in the Volpe killing. The detectives pointed out that the twenty-two ice-pick wounds indicated a revenge motive.

Bazzano reached New York four days after the Volpes were shot down, and registered at the Hotel Pennsylvania. The night of Aug. 7 he went to the Red Hook district of Brooklyn. In an empty store in that neighborhood—the police know the address but are withholding it—he was killed. His body was found next morning.

Photographs of the mutilated face were taken by the Brooklyn Homicide Squad under Captain John McGowan and copies of it were sent all over the East. When it reached Pittsburgh Bazzano's picture was recognized by his brother-in-law, Andrew Zapella of Pittsburgh, who came here to identify the body. That was on Aug. 11.

Since then Captain McGowan's men have been studying hotel registers and following other leads that led to the arrests yesterday morning. Between midnight and dawn, in various hotels and private dwellings in Manhattan and Brooklyn, they took into custody a total of nineteen suspects. Four women and one man were later released.

Report Murder-Feast Plan.

At the line-up in Police Headquarters the fourteen suspects denied all knowledge of the Bazzano murder. All maintained they were grocers or restaurant keepers. The nine from out of town said they were here to visit relatives. The police maintain they had assembled here for the murder feast to toast the Bazzano killers.

The police also said that they had information that the Bazzano murderers were to have been paid off at the dinner, something between $5,000 and $7,000, and that they were to be rewarded for their expertness with another assignment—the removal of "some big New York racketeer." The police were rather vague about this angle, however.

When the fourteen prisoners were arraigned before Magistrate Folwell in Brooklyn Homicide Court on a short affidavit, their counsel, Samuel Leibowitz, maintained that "the police have just rounded up everybody in sight." He said: "They have nothing on these men at all, and when the forty-eight hours are up they will be discharged in the same wholesale manner that they were brought in."

The fourteen men were held without bail for hearing Friday.

Seizure of 14 Calls Off Gang Murder Party

Prisoners Had Been Asked to Help Celebrate Bazzano Slaying, Police Say

Five Cities Represented

$5,000 Each Ready for 4 Killers, Officers Assert

There was to have been a party last night at a Manhattan hotel in celebration of the murder of John Bazzano, Pittsburgh underworld boss, whose stabbed and strangled body was left in a sack on Center Street, in the Red Hook section of Brooklyn, on August 8. Racketeers from Pittsburgh and Brooklyn, from Niagara Falls, Trenton and Buffalo had assembled here to do homage to the men who did away with Bazzano. But police learned about the impending celebration and early yesterday detectives rounded up fourteen of the invited guests. Under the circumstances the party is off.

Such Celebrations Not Unusual

Such celebrations, the police say, often follow an important killing. The idea behind the police activity was not to spoil the party but to teach the out-of-town gangsters to stay in their own backyards and to prevent further killings by the amalgamated forces.

The name of the hotel where the party was to have been staged, and certain other details, were not divulged by the detectives. However, the police claim to have information that the actual slayers of Bazzano, four in number, were to have been paid $5,000 each for their job, and were to have been offered that much or more to ambush a Manhattan racketeer who has been on the spot for some time and is no more liked by his fellows than was Bazzano.

List of Those Seized

The roll call of the fourteen arrested in the Bazzano case follows:

BROOKLYN: John Addo, known to the authorities as "Johnny Bath Beach"; Robert Anastasio, who passed eighteen months in Sing Sing death house before he gained a new trial and acquittal; Tony Bonasero, known as the "Chief"; Ciro Gallo and Joseph Traina.
PITTSBURGH: Santo Volpe, Carlo Sparlino, Michael Russo, Frank Adrano, Michael Bua and Angelo Colizza.
BUFFALO: Samuel Di Carlo, brother of Joseph Di Carlo, Buffalo's leading public enemy.
TRENTON: Peter Lombardi.
NIAGARA FALLS: Paul Palmeri.

The fourteen men were arrested in a series of raids between midnight and dawn. Police said some of the men were registered at three hotels in Manhattan and Brooklyn and others were picked up in night clubs and speakeasies. Altogether twenty prisoners, including two women, were taken, but six were released after questioning.

Police Explain Gang Custom

Police announced that the fourteen still held would be charged with conspiring to kill Bazzano in revenge for the killing of the three Volpe brothers, Pennsylvania liquor racketeers, who were ambushed in a Pittsburgh restaurant owned by Bazzano last July 25. Bazzano is said to have been lured to New York on a business deal and to have been wined and dined before he was put to death. The twenty-two stab wounds were explained on the ground that it is a gangster rule to compel all persons present at a killing to inflict at least one wound on the victim, to the end that all would be guilty and none would squeal.

Arraigned in Homicide Court, Brooklyn, on homicide charges, the fourteen prisoners pleaded not guilty and were held without bail for further hearing tomorrow. Samuel Leibowitz, their attorney, said:

"This is the most wholesale homicide arraignment in the history of criminal procedure in this country and it also will be the most wholesale discharge of defendants in the history of criminal procedure. There is nothing against these men—absolutely nothing."

Niagara Falls

In the early 1940s, Stephano Magaddino's ego and envy was about to cause complications for Papa. Stephano Magaddino was not one of Papa's friends. He had a lot of ego problems, as did many of his peers. A man needs to know his limitations. Papa was a special man. He had the whole package: intelligence, looks, respect and reputation. His popularity around the country led to the looming problem. Some Magaddino supporters tried to get Jimmy Guido to say he was sleeping with Mom, which would have brought shame to and discredited Papa. But Jimmy Guido had a special bond with Uncle Ernie, Dad and Uncle Frank. Magaddino's guys beat the piss out of Jimmy, but he would not break.

Papa received a call from Willie Moretti, who said, "Paul, there is going to be trouble. Get out of there." Willie, advising of the pending problem and explaining that with prohibition over there was nothing left in that one horse town (Buffalo and Niagara Falls) told Papa, "you don't need it, and we don't need it. We want you, and we need you here with us." I'm sure there was a lot of truth in Willie's words about the pending trouble. It was a good time and way to get him to move.

455 Passaic Avenue

New Jersey Rocks

In 1941, the Palmeris moved to Passaic, New Jersey. Papa wanted to buy a house, but Mama wanted no part of the responsibility. So they settled at 455 Passaic Avenue in a 4 bedroom, 2 bath art deco apartment with huge rooms and a foyer that comfortably accommodated their baby grand piano.

New Jersey was rocking, and in keeping with his ability to blend in, Papa and Mama became friends with their neighbors, Charlie Scuvuso, a Passaic detective and future chief of detectives, and his wife Connie. Don Paolo assumed his new role as intermediary to all the families nationally.

Under One Roof

Mama's mother (Maria Curti) lived with Mama and Papa, not with her husband. In Italian, grandmother is "Nona" — but we botched it to "Nono." Ironically, the reason she was estranged from Mama's father was because she did not believe in sex. She said she was not supposed to do such things. So I guess "Nono" was an appropriate name.

Nono and Papa were fond of each other and shared a love for cuisine. They would sit once a week and plan all the meals. Then Papa would do the shopping. Not only did he like to shop for groceries, but he could steal something, sometimes just a package of ham, but he felt fulfilled.

Nono died at 99, 1 month short of her 100th birthday. The day she died, Mom made me go into the room and look at her, to see how peaceful she was. Italians, especially my family, had a thing about death. I remember, growing up, the daily phone calls to discuss who died and the arrangements. I used to think wakes and funerals were the family's number one activity.

Aunt Marie also lived with Papa and Mama, before she got married in 1959. Then she and Uncle Ange lived there with Mama for a few years. In the 1960s, when Aunt Marie and Uncle Ange moved out into their own place, Mama downsized to a one bedroom apartment in the same building.

The Last Envelope

After Papa died, every Friday afternoon, there was a knock on Mama's door. There stood Tony Scomo with her weekly envelope. This lasted for 12 years. Also there were periodic payments, collected from his debtors. This was unheard of, but Papa's friends made sure his widow was taken care of, and that his death did not exonerate his debtors.

Ironically enough, 35 years later, while I was attempting to collect money in Florida, the mother-in-law of the guy I was trying to collect from asked me where I was from. When I told her northern New Jersey, she asked me if I knew Tony Scomo. 35 years later, I'm sure he was dead, and if not what did he have to do with the current situation?

In 1967, I was nineteen and it was Sunday morning. So I set forth on my Sunday job, going to Passaic to pick up Mama for dinner. Sometimes I would laugh, thinking it was a big step up from my bread carrying job for Papa.

That morning, as we rode in the car, I knew there was something wrong so I asked her, "What was the matter, Mama?"

"Costello came over this morning," Mama said.

"I made him coffee. He was somber. He handed me an envelope and he said, 'Signora, the young guys won't approve any more payments. This is the last of Paul's share."

I reminded her, "You know what Mama, he still gets respect. Costello came personally to see you."

"I know, Lou Lou, I know," Mama said.

And for all those so-called experts that said Frank Costello was retired, oh well.

The Queen

I think things have changed, definitely for the worst. The way the women are today, the way they act and speak make me cringe. A reality TV show like MOB WIVES, where every other word is bleeped, is the antithesis of Mama and the women I grew up with.

If you want to know what Mama was like, think "class" not "crass." For example, I went with my wife to see the movie *The Queen*. In one scene, the queen and the queen mum were sitting in a room, knees together, and purses next to them.

I turned to my wife and said, "Who do they remind you of?" She replied, "Your mother, grandmother, and aunts. They were ladies and the men were gentlemen."

Mama died on September 15, 1998, at the age of 101.

Mama at 89

Connections

MICHAEL. My father made him an offer he couldn't refuse.

KAY. What was that?

MICHAEL. Luca Brasi held a gun to his head and my father assured him that either his brains or his signature would be on the contract.

KAY. (Speechless)

MICHAEL. That's a true story. ... That's my family Kay, that's not me.

From the wedding scene in movie THE GODFATHER (1972)

One of the Boys

Among ourselves, the terms we used to describe mob guys were: "He's one of the boys," or "He's connected," or "He's a Ma Haffer."

Or with gestures. The person describing the person's affiliation would make two fists, thumbs extended, and use a motion, repeatedly moving the thumbs away from and toward the chest or lapels, symbolically saying, "Look at me, I'm important." Or, using the index finger and thumb to pinch and wave the collar, signifying a button or badge, synonymous for Made.

Castellammarese War

Castellammare del Golfo, Italy ("Castle by the Sea") is a town in the Trapani Province of Sicily. In the early 1950s, famed English author Gavin Maxwell wrote about Castellammare. According to Maxwell, 80% of the male population had spent time in jail and 30% had committed murder. Striking statistics for a town with a population of 10,000.

Castellammare is where Buffalo Bill and Papa were born, along with other Sicilians who immigrated to the US. They were connected through their heritage, ambition and need to rise above discrimination.

According to historians, the "Castellammarese War" erupted in 1930 when Salvatore Maranzano, boss of the Castellammarese-aligned faction in New York State, was challenged by New York City-based boss of bosses Giuseppe "Joe the Boss" Masseria, who decided that the Castellammarese leaders in the U.S. were inciting rebellion against his administration. Masseria imposed a death sentence against the Castellammarese faction and a war between the factions erupted. Masseria was opposed in New York by forces led by Maranzano and a group of young, soon to be powerful mobsters, led by Charles "Lucky" Luciano, who formed an alliance between his men and Maranzano, which led to Joe the Boss's assassination in the spring of 1931. Maranzano briefly served as Mafia boss of bosses until his own assassination.

Wild West

In 1870 in Texas (and the West in general, amidst the booze, gambling, prostitution and the virtual cornucopia of vice and lawlessness), men wore guns and shot each other at the drop of their ten gallon hats. This behavior continued through the 1920s.

My ancestors and their friends came from a similar atmosphere in Sicily. They only shot and killed amongst themselves. They conducted business in cities with paved roads and concrete sidewalks surrounded by so-called civilized and sophisticated people. They were visibly noticed, unlike in the frontier towns with wood plank walks and dirt roads inhabited by cowboys, farmers, ranchers and miners, who faded into the scenery. As for my boyhood heroes, like so many occupations playing in a big media town, the money was great, but it will get you considerably more attention. Not so good.

Mob Culture

Standard operating procedure for historians is to mount a case for their beliefs or claims. Obviously, the farther away from the date or subject matter, the more room for skewed accuracy. While way too much emphasis has been, and still is, placed on the mob's power structure, unbeknownst to Salvatore Maranzano, his Roman Legion model not only formed the modern day Mafia, it actually became a model for franchising and multi- level marketing.

Look at the structure from the bottom up. If a citizen should be in an enterprise that either begins to make money or is seemingly infringing on an associate or Made Guy's interests, the citizen will at some point be coerced into paying a fee (MOB TAX) in order to continue to do business. Not unlike all the other licenses and fees they already pay. And in most cases, he will see an increase in business and he will be patronized by people who want to do business with a Connected business. The fees collected in this or any other enterprise starts with the Associate to the Made Guy, who kicks up to his Capo, and then to the Boss.

As with a franchise or multi — level business, the top producers still earn the lion's share. The best insurance for any level, short of the Boss, is to be a top earner. As with any other lifestyle, money brings respect, whether warranted or not.

Earning is and always will be number one. In light of the current crop of Made Men, a ceremony with finger pricking and burning prayer cards with saints' pictures is ludicrous. Especially when ranking guys and Bosses flip. Meanwhile, the dollars are enormous compared to the 1920s through the 70s, and why not? Look at other types of earnings: business professionals, athletes, celebrities, etc. The big problem for Organized Crime and the Honored Society is long, long and in some cases life sentences. It was always believed that someone would rise to the top, pull everybody together, and control profitability. Realizing the fact that you could be taken out by a friend or blood relative, or be facing life in a 6x8 foot cell with 1 hour per day out of the cell and two showers a week, does not bode well for the code of *omerta* (vow of silence).

Mob Guys used to stand out amongst other businessmen, doctors, lawyers and assorted professionals. They were the best dressed and groomed and boldly shouted success. I subscribe to the adage "clothes make the man". Look at the current photos, the men and the women supposedly in the life look like they belong in a flea market. Far from the well-dressed men I looked up to and the women in their lives. In today's relaxed society, more people dress business casual, but unfortunately, compared to the old pictures of people in The Life, they look like Goodwill was their couturier. With all the criticism of John Gotti, he was always well dressed, even when he was casual, and the people around him looked similar. Those days are gone along with their wit. When John Gotti was boarding the plane for the United

States Penitentiary at Marion, Illinois, where he would spend the remainder of his life, he said, 'You think it's too late to say, 'I'm sorry?'

Generosity

There has been a lot written about all the old time guys, but they never write about their generosity, like Buffalo Bill. Everybody around them in any capacity was taken care of.

In Niagara Falls, part of Papa's popularity in the Italian community came from his good deeds. Like his brother Angelo, he helped the less fortunate, organizing busloads of people to picnics and trips to Canadian beaches. For many, it was their only recreation. Papa shared his good fortune, as did many of his peers.

Willie Moretti fed a lot of people. He ensured all of the people around him were financially OK — waiters, shoe shine boys, newsstand operators, etc. He was responsible for hundreds of people's welfare.

Willie, as with most of his contemporaries was charming, gentlemanly and had a great sense of humor.

He loved practical jokes and pushing the envelope.

On an extremely hot summer day, while he was having a discussion with a few of his guys, he turned to two of his enforcers and told them to make themselves useful and "go get some ice cream cones". They immediately hopped to and shortly returned with several cones. Willie purposely continued his discussion while the ice cream dripped all over their hands knowing nobody would talk or act until he was done. He finally couldn't keep a straight face and burst into his hardy laugh, breaking the ice. Everybody joined in the laugh and grabbed a cone, a little soft and runny, but everybody had a good laugh.

I don't know the year but Willie had been banned from Monmouth Park raceway. He sent scouts to find the best vantage point to watch a race from outside the track and would go and sit outside to be close to the action.

He would give Dad his sheets to tally and when Dad reported if the results were favorable Willie would hand him $100. Talk about supplemental income!

I've mentioned everybody's generosity, but Willie's was most notable. If anything good or bad happened to someone close to him he responded with a $100 bill and his congratulations or condolences. It's not that he was by any means shy or at a loss for words. He believed the gift would help celebrate or ease the pain.

Santo Volpe became the president of Volpe Coal Company and was active in the coal industry nationally and Pennsylvania politics.

Santo Volpe personally saw to it that all the miners and their families had groceries when they were on strike. Naturally, He shared his success with his family first and his friends second, but the general population was always included.

Volpe's daughters, Tina and Angela, were married on the same day. In addition to the lavish double reception in the US, he also served the same meal to everybody in his hometown of Montedoro in Sicily. Then, he had a train car with two bedrooms and a parlor outfitted, and told the two couples to travel to their hearts' content on their honeymoons.

A WISER GUY

When my parents married, Mr. Volpe sent sterling flatware for 12 as a gift. At the reception, he handed Dad an envelope with a key to a hotel suite at the Waldorf Astoria and a note. They could stay as long as they wanted. They stayed a week. Dad said he could not pay for a newspaper, a pack of cigarettes, shoe shine, or tip anybody. It was all on Mr. Volpe. Not bad for a man who came to America in steerage, with 3 cents in his pocket.

But generosity does not make you immune from harm.

The Waldorf-Astoria

Dear Anna & Joe:—

This is the key that locks the two hearts in one chest

With the help of God we wish you happiness, good health and long life.

Dorothea & Santo

Goombada Willie

Guarino "Willie" Moretti (A/K/A Willie Moore) was known to us as "Goombada Willie," which is Sicilian for Godfather, the term of respect. His wife's name was Angela, but we all called her "Goomada." Until my teens, I thought that was her name. When I reflect, I was wise beyond my years, but so naïve, especially when I remember Mama and Mrs. Moretti referring to each other as Goomada. I was about three and a half when Goombada Willie died. I have vague recollection of him.

Willie is probably best known because he was immortalized in *The Godfather* scene, "He made him an offer he couldn't refuse" — referring to Willie getting Frank Sinatra out of his personal service contract with Tommy Dorsey.

Willie was old, old school in his loyalties and friendships. Vito Genovese wanted to assume what he believed was his rightful place as head of the Luciano Family. In order to accomplish this, he had to remove Frank Costello. Genovese knew if any harm came to Costello, there would be no way to subdue Willie Moore. Willie had worked for Buffalo Bill in Niagara Falls and he and Papa became the closest of friends.

LOUIS P DIVITA

I know a lot of guys with steel balls, but long before the world heard of titanium, Willie's balls were made of it. Case in point, as Willie and Pete LaPlaca were leaving the Lincoln Bar on Henry Street in Passaic, a car sped around the corner, shooting. Without any hesitation, Willie and Pete dropped to one knee, returning fire. They were breaking in a new driver who, after the melee, they found crouched on the floor. Pete dragged him out of the car, confirmed the kid had not been hit, told him to find a ride, got behind the wheel and drove off.

F78 ORGANIZEID CRIME IN INTERSTATE COMMERCE

TESTIMONY OF THEODORE MOEICI, M. D., PASSAIC, N. J., ACCOM-

PANIED BY JOHN T. SULLIVAN, NEW YORK, N. Y.

Mr. Halley. Do yon know the names of the nurses who are on the case?

Dr. MoRici. Yes. One is Miss Lyons and the other one is Estelle —

I don't know the last name.

Dr. Morici & The Kefauver Hearings

In 1950, the heat was on. The Kefauver Hearings were underway. (This was a special Senate Committee investigating organized crime. Senator Estes Kefauver was Committee Chairman.)

Dr. Theodore Morici was our next door neighbor when we lived on Howe Avenue in Passaic. He liked me and would ask Mom to have me join his family for lunch regularly. They ate their big meal at noon and there were generally eight to ten people every day.

Dr. Morici was the chief surgeon at Beth Israel Hospital, a good doc to have on the payroll.

During the Kefauver Hearings, Dr. Morici was subpoenaed to testify. Kefauver questioned the doctor as to Willie Moretti's health issues and his inability to take the stand. Dr Morici, coincidently, wrote a note saying that Joe Adonis couldn't testify because he had to care for his ill wife. Kefauver even exposed Miss Lyons, Dr. Morici's nurse. The doctor claimed, under oath, that she had to help in Mrs. A's care .YEAH RIGHT!

Willie's Catholic Funeral

Most people who knew WILLIE knew the good. After Willie's death on October 4, 1951, to make matters worse for his family and close allies, the pastor of Corpus Christi Roman Catholic Church in Hasbrouck Heights was refusing to give Willie a Catholic burial. This caused Papa to visit the pastor. When Papa arrived, the priest offered his condolences and explained the church policy regarding funerals for those in THE LIFE.

Papa called on his negotiating skills and reminded the priest that every Sunday morning, as Willie sat in the front pew with his wife and three daughters and deposited large sums of cash in the collection basket, the priest never questioned his occupation. When Willie was the one-man building committee and built the church, the priest never cast aspersions on his generosity. But now, when the church has nothing left to gain, they chose to distance themselves.

Papa explained to the pastor that this mass and funeral service was not optional. He was very persuasive. Goombada Willie was buried with all the rights of the Catholic Church.

Former Falls Man Material Witness In Murder Case

One-time Funeral Home Operator Here And Fair Lawn Man Taken in Custody, Jailed Without Bail by Jersey Police

A former well-known Niagara Falls resident, Paul Palmieri, 58, of Passaic, N. J., was taken into custody by New Jersey police yesterday and is being held with another man as a material witness in the recent slaying of Racketeer Willie Moretti.

Palmieri, a native of Italy, spent more than 20 years here before moving to Passaic about ten years ago and operated a funeral home in Pine avenue for several years. He formerly resided at 1538 Whitney avenue.

PAUL PALMIERI

Taken into custody with Palmieri was Ralph Belvedere, 40, of Fair Lawn, N. J. Both men are being held without bail.

Deputy Attorney General Harry L. Towe said yesterday the men, former cronies of Moretti, could give the state "valuable information."

Belvedere is part owner of a Lodi N. J., tavern, "The Blue Flame," located in Route 6. Palmeri's son, Frank, is married to one of Moretti's three daughters.

The two men, held in Bergen county jail without bail, were not actual witnesses to Moretti's murder, Towe emphasized, but are material witnesses in the case.

Towe, in charge of the Bergen county prosecutor's office, said the pair could supply information on Moretti's activities before he was shot to death in a Clifside Park restaurant October 4.

He said the arrests stemmed from the tracing of telephone calls Moretti made from the restaurant the night before the shooting.

Belvedere and Palmieri were questioned for almost five hours yesterday. Neither of them had been questioned by police before that.

The deputy attorney general said the men were "very uncooperative" during the questioning, but added, "we know damn sure that they can tell us more than they have."

Both Have Police Records

They were arrested at their homes by state troopers. Both of them have police records, Towe said.

The state has made no arrests of suspects in the slaying of the talkative gambler. Four men, seen in the restaurant just before Moretti was shot twice in the head, have not been identified.

Towe said Belvedere, once a strongarm man for Moretti, split with the gambler several years ago for reasons not known.

Palmieri's son and daughter-in-law live in a Hasbrouck Heights, N. J., home, which Moretti is reported to have provided for them.

In Demand as Speaker

Palmieri has a police record in this city, having been indicted by the Niagara county grand jury for second degree assault in connection with an alleged attack on Patrolman Thomas Nickerson in May, 1934. He was arrested for assault in Buffalo in 1914 and was arrested in Chicago in 1931 in connection with a kidnaping there.

In 1932 he was involved in a homicide investigation in New York City but was released after questioning.

While here Palmieri had a reputation as an orator in the Italian language and was in demand as a speaker at various functions. He was said to have studied law at an Italian university before coming to this country.

The Deal House

In the summer of 1958, when I was 10, we went to Goomada's house in Deal, New Jersey. That was the house Goombada Willie always referred to, and it became a focal point of the Kefauver investigations when he told the Committee of Congressmen, "Don't forget my house in Deal. If you are down on the shore, you are invited."

We drove down and spent the day at the beach. Later that afternoon, back at the house there was a knock on the door. When Goomada went to answer the door, she saw police all over the front yard. She told the adults to get us kids upstairs. As I watched from the balcony with a couple of my cousins, Goomada, with Mama by her side, handled the situation masterfully.

The local police had called the New Jersey state troopers and surrounded the house. Why? Because the locals saw a lot of Cadillacs parked at the house. Willie was dead for seven years. What were they thinking? Besides, if Willie was alive they would never have bothered him.

Well, the locals thought they hit the jackpot. See, the infamous Appalachian Meeting Debacle in Appalachian, NY was on November 14, 1957. It's kind of amazing when you think about it. In 1958, a lot of Cadillacs parked at the home of a deceased mobster could draw the full raid-ready attention of the New Jersey state troopers. Could you imagine if they would have forced their way in to the house, only to find a band of sinister women and children?

Moe Brown

Mob Structure; Boss, Underboss, Consigliere (consular advisor), Capo (Captain Skipper), Soldier, Associate.

Among the Associates, a phenomenon in Mob Life is the "Hanger On" who sometimes elevates through attrition, sometimes he just stays put, and sometimes he has power at the pleasure of the Boss. Hangers On are a friendly, trustworthy, go-to for simple non-criminal and /or non-dangerous tasks. I knew dozens of these guys. They're safe because they never interfere or cross anybody, they befriend and help everybody, and they never pose a threat.

One such guy was Frank (Moe Brown) Sesta, a close friend of Uncle Ernie's. Moe Brown was a cutter in a garment factory, and as the story goes, he was the fastest and best in the business. Like so many people in and or around The Life, that was his straight job. He fell under the Genovese banner, specifically Willie, and in 1933 he was one of the leaders in the Bread and Unity strike, when 70,000 workers walked out for a fair wages and hours.

Moe always sent Mama Flowers on Mother's Day. His classic comment was at a wedding I attended. I was talking to a couple of my cousins when he approached. After we exchanged greetings,

Moe said, "Louis you married a nationality, right?" referring to my wife's Lebanese heritage.

In the 1990s, at the appeals hearing of Louis "Streaky" Gato and Al "Little Al" Greco, Moe Brown's name came up. While Arthur Belli was in jail, Little Al took over the Belli brothers' gambling operation and told Robert Belli things were going to be different. Shortly thereafter, Robert's hot dog truck was blown up and he was beaten up by two men with baseball bats. Later, Arthur disappeared after his release from prison because he was supposedly planning to take back his book.

Moe Brown was asked to take Robert Belli to a meeting with Streaky and Little Al's defense counsel. Moe took Robert to a job interview the day before the trial, and discussed the case on numerous occasions saying, "Isn't it a shame about Little Al and this case." Moe pressed Belli to let an associate drive him to a pre-trial hearing, but Belli declined, instead taking a ride from a government investigator and asking the investigator to run the associate's license plate.

Belli testified that Moe Brown had been in the courtroom during his testimony, standing in the back directly in front of him, and that Moe looked unhappy. You see, Moe was standing right in the line of Belli's vision and there were plenty of seats. Moe Brown is not an intimidating person. Moe Brown was in the court room as a representative. He was there as a reminder. He was in the courtroom to deliver a message.

Jimmy Guido

Jimmy (Bunny) Guido returned to Niagara Falls after WW2 and hooked up with some buddies .They started building houses and made a fortune.

In the early fifties, there was a nail shortage in the US and the price of nails was skyrocketing. Builders would pay anything for nails. What did they care? It was a pass through. Jimmy had ties in Italy who told him they could supply the demand.

Jimmy and his partners, in an attempt to dominate the nail business, let greed get the best of them. They pooled their dollars and waited for the shipment and the impending windfall. Unfortunately, they got screwed. Nails were sold in barrels. When the shipment arrived they opened the barrels. Surprise, they were 1/8 full of nails on top of scrap metal.

Poor Jimmy never rebounded. He was a great salesman, made a good living but was always coming up with another Make A Million plan. In his later life, Uncle Frank took him under his wing and watched over him until his unexpected death

Easy Time

I always laugh at the myth that Wise Guys do easy time or are treated differently in jail. There are FBI communications from taped conversations between Tommy (Ryan) Eboli's brother Pat and Mike Genovese, brother of Vito Genovese, concerning a column by Walter Winchell regarding the removal of a prisoner in Atlanta federal penitentiary from the general population, with the speculation the person removed was a mob defector whose information was far more damaging than that of Joe Valachi.

They decided to reach out to Pete LaPlaca to ascertain whether the Winchell column had validity. Pat and Mike needed to know the truth. The report further stated that the long cafeteria style tables were removed and replaced with tables for four and prisoners may eat with whomever they please. I guess they weren't staying in the Presidential Suite!

The Federal Correctional Institution, Ray Brook New York, was constructed as a prison; the first occupants were Olympians competing in the *1980 Winter Olympics*, in Lake Placid.

Uncle Ernie was in Ray Brook. While it was built as a prison, other than the razor barb, it wasn't that bad. But he was subjected to cavity searches and could only eat the meals they served, no food from the outside. And when he was on work release, he never took a chance, "cause you can't trust nobody". The food sucked, so he lived on cookies and other vending machine fare. All the guys I knew who did "a bid" had similar stories. So much for the steak and lobster scene in Goodfellas.

During Ernie's stay he took charge and posted a sign reserving the TV for a Frank Sinatra concert. When he entered the TV room to watch the concert, the room was occupied by a group of young black inmates watching the TV. When Ernie asked in his sarcastic tone if they had trouble reading the reserved sign, their reply was, "sorry we didn't know it was you, we don't want any trouble with you Italian guys "as they promptly left the room. Posture and Image!

When Uncle Ange went to visit him and people inquired why he was going to Lake Placid, he would tell them he was visiting his brother in law who was an ice skater

While Ernie was in prison he made friends with other Wise Guys from around the country. One in particular was Joseph (Chickie) Ciancaglini, Sr., a ranking member from Philly who helped Ernie adapt to prison life. That was in 1983. Chickie is currently due to be released in 2015.

The Family

Mom

My mother, Anna (Anne) Palmeri, was Mama and Papa's oldest child. When Mom was 5 years old, Mama dressed her and sent her off to school. Mom promptly returned home with a note pinned to her jacket. The note said, "When your daughter speaks English she will be admitted to school."

That night, Mama told Papa they could only speak English in the house so the kids could learn the language. They were all bilingual. Unfortunately for my generation, our parents spoke only English. Until they didn't want us to know what was going on, then they resorted to Italian.

Mom was way ahead of her time. If she were born in the late 1930s or 40s, she would have probably been encouraged to go to college and could very well have become a prominent professional or business woman. She had more strength than most men, a cunning instinct (ESP) and the posture of the "manor born." She was exposed to The Life at an early age and what she saw was the good side. Unlike the liars that claim they didn't know what their fathers did, she had a good idea. Besides, if she didn't, how would she know who's who and what's what?

All the exposure never swayed her from being the quintessential lady, as was Mama and all my aunts. The worst word I ever heard any of them utter was "damn." No matter what the situation, they never dropped their guard.

She wanted me to be fully versed on our history and encouraged me to help all the family, especially Ernie. Unlike Mama, Mom had no mixed feelings for Louis future. It was to be college and white collar all the way. Mom was my number one advocate and cheerleader followed by Mama, Aunt Marie and Dad.

L eft to Right: Mama, Dad, and Mom

Dad

My father, Joseph (Joe) DiVita, knew Anne Palmeri since their childhood in Niagara Falls. The Palmeris and DiVitas were family friends for years. Mama said she knew Dad from when he was two years old

Dad & The Chinamen

My father was 16 years old, tending bar in his father's saloon, when Papa walked in.

Papa: Good morning Joe.

Dad: Good morning Mr. Palmeri.

Papa: Joe, two men are going to come and ask for me. Send them to the back.

Dad: Sure, Mr. Palmeri.

Later, Two Chinamen walk in and up to the bar, carrying a basket.

Dad: What do you want?

Chinese: We are here to see the man called Paul.

Dad: He's in the back.

Fifteen minutes later the Chinamen leave without the basket.

Chinese: Thank you.

Dad: OK.

Fifteen minutes later, Papa comes out with the basket, and places a $5 bill on the bar.

Papa: Thank you, Joe. My regards to your mother and father.

Dad: Yes sir, thank you Mr. Palmeri.

As Dad said later, "that basket wasn't filled with Easter eggs."

The DiVitas

Dad's father was Louis N DiVita. He had two brothers, Uncle Jack and Uncle Joe. They were in the bar and restaurant business. The brothers' one big opportunity was when they started The DiVita Macaroni Company. Uncle Joe was the Managing Partner and while Louis and Jack worked their restaurants and "SPEAKS," Uncle Joe screwed up DiVita Macaroni and they lost their opportunity.

They made a decent living but never made a score. As mentioned previously, they were friends with the Palmeris. Louis died from pneumonia when Dad was 16 so he quit high school to help his mother maintain the business.

Uncle Louis was too young to work the bar and Dad's older brother Sam was married with a baby, and besides, had a good paying job at a pharmacy. Unfortunately for Uncle Sam, he never finished school so he couldn't get his own license. He died suddenly and unexpectedly in his forties.

Dad and Uncle Louis were both in the service during WWII. Dad was in the Air Force and Louis was in the Army. While they were overseas their mother ran the business by herself with the little help Sammy could provide. After the war, Dad spent a little time in Niagara Falls helping his mother and brother Louis until he married Mom and moved to New Jersey.

Dad's mother Philomena Minnie (Grand Ma DeDe) DiVita nee Mazzei was like so many woman of her era. Unlike Mama, she did her own domestic work and when her husband was alive she made daily specials for the restaurant. With her husband gone she wore all the hats while her sons were away. Stephano Magaddino made her buy cases of cordials in order to be able to buy hard liquor. When Dad returned home, he went to Papa who said let it go. While it was a typical Magaddino move, it wasn't worth giving him the satisfaction of letting him know you were bothered by his actions. Dad gave away the cases a bottle at a time to their patrons. Revenge was sweet. When Grand Ma DeDe died, they made arrangements with The Rooney Funeral Home, which had to chap Stephano's small-minded ass.

During World War II, Mom and Dad corresponded by letters. After they were married, they settled in Hasbrouck Heights, New Jersey.

Dad went to work for Willie Moretti, driving for the games (Gambling Dens) and working the phones in the wire room. And Papa would use him to drive to important meetings and stand guard — something he did not relish, but had to do. Unlike Papa and Uncle Ernie, Dad was not comfortable carrying a gun.

Once, when he was stopped by the cops, he hid his gun under the car seat. The cop told Dad to have his boss call him, referring to Willie. Nothing else came of that stop, but it was a nerve-wracking experience for Dad.

Because I was an ambitious, polite, articulate kid and mature beyond my years, most adults liked me and held me in high esteem. Dad, while he was extremely proud, was aware of my dangerous side. He would brag about my accomplishments, but chastise me when he knew I did something. I was pretty good at keeping things from him.

Dad was not cut out for The Life and his reservations probably kept me somewhat level-headed and prevented me from going off the deep end. Remember, he was there in the glory days. And because of Papa, he was next to all the big names, and those who were smart enough NOT to be big names. As a teenager and young man at family gatherings and visits with friends, I would relish the respect and friendship Dad had, even though his stock devalued when Papa died.

Dad followed the more legitimate path but he maintained his friendships with the Boys, and when an occasional opportunity presented itself, he never turned down a favor, especially if it included a payday. But I felt bad for him. He was a trusting man, not a good trait. Especially when one of the first things I was taught was, "Don't Trust Nobody" and "Always Know Who's in The Room Next to You," which simply means don't do anything with anybody who could flip. Which refers back to "Don't Trust Nobody."

Anyway, Dad had a good, respectable job at American Express. His boss, Charlie Lenox, who Dad thought was his friend, flipped, put Dad as the architect, and took him down. Dad was never the same. Dad, Charlie, Uncle Bunny and others were doing something with traveler's checks. Dad told me who was involved, but of course he did the right thing and never gave anybody up. He took the fall, but he got lucky. Apparently Amex didn't want the publicity and Dad skated. Another reason he was always worried about what I was doing.

Back Row, Left to Right: Dad's Aunt Rose, Dad, Mom, Unknown (Hidden), Grandma Dede, Uncle Sam, Aunt Laura, and Cousin Tommy Divita. Front Row, Left To Right: Cousin Tim and Cousin Carl. Picture from Uncle Louis' Wedding

1955 World Series

October 8, 1955. We all waited anxiously for Dad to come home from Yankee Stadium. He was invited to attend a World Series game by his old Niagara Falls buddy, Sal Maglie, who was pitching against the NY Yankees. Dad sat with Sal's wife and watched as Sal pitched a 5 hitter and allowed only 2 runs. Only to witness Sal lose to Don Larsen, who pitched the historical perfect game.

Lucille Ball

Dad's cousin, Johnny Devita, was Lucille Ball's flame. While much was written and speculated, she always referred to her love for Johnny. In fact, she supposedly took Desi to meet Johnny in 1956. Dad often spoke of the time Lucy spent with his family.

Johnny Devita spelled his name differently than we did. There are a lot of Devitos and Devitas. I think he caved under the pressure of always correcting people. To this day, I have to be explicit and say "DiVita, Capital D as in David, small I, Capital V as in Victor, small ita."

Aunt Marie and the cousins. That's me on the far right.

Aunt Marie & Uncle Ange

Marie Palmeri was Mom's younger sister. Aunt Marie worked at Passaic Clifton National Bank, which later became New Jersey Bank and Trust. But her real job was being there for the family.

During the big 1957 Christmas celebration, Angelo Petricca was a new face among family and friends. Two years later, he became Uncle Ange when he married Aunt Marie. While she focused her attention on her husband, she always had time for everyone in the family, and with Uncle Ange, supported the efforts of my brother Joe, sister Anne and myself. We affectionately tell Aunt Marie stories. It's funny, but her identity to everyone, including my wife's former business partner and our friends, was "Aunt Marie."

As my Godmother, Aunt Marie paid special attention to me. Before Uncle Ange, Aunt Marie took me to see the Hopalong Cassidy Rodeo and the Ringling Brothers Circus, both at Madison Square Garden. In 1957, after I was hit by a car while riding my bike, she spent her vacation taking me places to break the monotony. Even though it was the late 1950s, prior to their marriage, when Aunt Marie wanted to cook for Uncle Ange, I was the strategically placed chaperone at their dinner dates.

Their wedding was a big event for all the kids. There was no way Aunt Marie was getting married without her nieces and nephews. We all wore summer tuxes, white dinner jackets with black tuxedo pants and cummerbunds. The girls wore flared dresses. Big Paul and myself were the altar boys.

Would you believe, right before the wedding, the priest shook down Uncle Ange to pay the altar boys from the parish for showing up? It wouldn't have happened if Uncle Ernie had been in the sacristy, but he was in the vestibule getting ready to walk Aunt Marie down the aisle and give her away.

Anyway, we all had a great time and she was so happy when she had her nieces and nephews on the dance floor doing the Hokey Pokey. She was all about family.

Actions speak louder than words. Uncle Ange showed his affection for me, taking me with him to different places, most of the time no place special, just hanging out or to get something to eat. Marie and Ange never had children, so they always went overboard for all the cousins, but were especially generous with Joe, Anne and me. They were always looking out for my welfare and when I moved to Florida, Uncle Ange was responsible for hooking me up with Mario Goffredo.

When Aunt Marie died in 2010, it was a blow to all, and she is missed by my family.

Uncle Don

Dominick LaPlaca, "Uncle Don," was the son of Peter (Lodi Pete) LaPlaca, who was Willie Moretti's right-hand man. Don married Rose Moretti, Willie's middle daughter. Both Uncle Don and Aunt Rose were very fond of Mom and Dad, and the feeling was mutual, hence they asked Uncle Don to be my Godfather, an honor reserved for someone who is deserving of the highest level of respect and trust.

Uncle Don was not only tailored for the position, but assumed the role with full responsibility. See, according to tradition, if something were to happen to the parents, the godparents would assume the responsibility of raising the child. The designation of the title Godfather was adopted to signify one who watches over, guards, protects and helps with the individual's welfare and assures their participation in the Catholic religion.

Considering he was young in years, Uncle Don was old school in traditions. As a child, Don was taught to hunt, play golf, and was a man's man. He boxed in military prep school and his stature told you not to try him. He was friends with a lot of important people, celebrities, and professional athletes. He had an audience with Pope Pius XII and the Pope gave him a medal with his likeness and blessed it. Uncle Don gave the medal to me, but unfortunately it disappeared from my locker during gym in the ninth grade. Whoever took it was smart enough to never tell anybody for fear of the consequences.

Uncle Don's love for fighting led to a friendship with Rocky Marciano (Rocco Francis Marchegiano), the world heavy weight champion, who trained at the Long Pond Inn in Green Wood Lake, NY. When I was in my teens and the legal age for drinking in New Jersey was 21, we would go across the state line to drink at the Long Pond.

From the age of five, whenever I saw Uncle Don, after the traditional kiss hello, he would take his stance, square off and tell me to "put 'em up" and show me a new punch or combination.

New Year's Eve, 1961, after having our annual New Year's Eve Chinese dinner, Mom, Dad, Joe, Anne and myself headed to Uncle Don's New Year's Party. This night, my greeting wasn't any different, except when he squared off, he caught a picture on the piano that flew off and hit me across the bridge of my nose. It left me with a scar that I carry to this day.

Like all the women I was around, Aunt Rose was a marvelous cook and she and Uncle Don loved to entertain. Uncle Don had just completed his dream home in Upper Saddle River NJ. It was an architectural masterpiece, set on heavily wooded acreage. While the elevation showed a sprawling ranch, upon entering the house at the back of the foyer was a triple wide staircase with a few steps up to the bedrooms.

This house had everything you could ever want for living, entertaining and comfort. The crowning glory was, because of the length of the house, he contracted to have a custom steel support beam fabricated to eliminate the need for lolly columns. Why?

So he could install two automatic pin setters in the basement for his own bowling alley. At that time, they cost seventy five hundred dollars apiece. Pretty pricy, considering a new Cadillac cost between five and six thousand, depending on the model.

At midnight on that New Years, after all the kissing, hugging and crying (for the deceased, of course) — the men in my family, like many Italian men, fired their guns. Uncle Don gave me three spent shells. At the time, I did not realize the significance that scar on my nose or those gun shells would have.

Late that night, as we were pulling away from the house, Uncle Don waved bye from his front porch, snow on the ground, with no coat on. Mom said affectionately, "Look at that jerk, he's going to catch his death of cold."

The next morning, Mom and Dad were making breakfast when the phone rang. Dad answered and started to tear. He hung up, sobbing, "Donnie's dead." He was helping Aunt Rose clean up from the party when he fell off a chair with a major heart attack. Dead at 39 years old.

Uncle Ernie

Ernesto/Ernest ("Ernie") Palmeri was the oldest son, and a man of Papa's stature and prominence had to deal with his antics. Most people liked Ernie. He had a gift: he could take your last buck, but you never felt he robbed you. Growing up, I always was conflicted about The Life. It's a hard decision which path to take when the people around you are, shall we say, animated and colorful.

In my adult life, I met numerous people who had dealings with Uncle Ernie. Some loved him, some accepted or tolerated him, but all agreed he was a character. Wild is probably an underrated adjective to describe him. He had a serious side, a comic side and a dark side.

Young Ernie

Mama said, "When Ernie was a baby, I put him in the carriage in front of the house to get fresh air. Then, I heard a dog barking." Mama ran to the door and found a German Shepherd pouncing, overturning the carriage, with baby Ernie crying. She used a broom to swing at the dog, who ran to the yard next door. Of course, Mama told Papa all about it.

Mama said, "Papa was furious. So he made a MEATBALL." Papa threw the meatball over the fence. The dog ate it and died.

Later, when Papa came home, he found the man next door in his front yard, crying. Papa greeted his neighbor and asked what was wrong. The neighbor said he found his dog dead in the backyard. The man carried on about his "best friend" (his dog.) And Papa offered his condolences.

"You're a good friend, Mr. Palmeri," said the neighbor. Papa nodded and smiled. Papa's ability to show empathy and conduct himself as an educated gentleman contributed to his popularity and his cover, both in business and personal matters.

Uncle Ernie died after a short illness. While he was in the hospital, he was visited by all of his children as well as Mom, Uncle Frank and Aunt Marie. Big Elena said everybody who came to visit parked in different places every day, as would be expected, and nobody noticed a Catholic church. After Ernie died, everybody leaving the hospital was stunned to hear Church bells. Big Elena said if anyone could make that happen it was Ernie. Kinda makes you wonder about the German Shepherd.

As Ernie grew up, trouble followed. When he was a teenager, Papa read him the riot act about sneaking out or coming home past curfew. At one point, Papa said, "Ernie, the next time you disobey my rules I will kill you."

When Ernie would sneak out or miss curfew, he would throw pebbles at Mom's bedroom window to wake her up and she would open the front door for him. But one night, she was no help because she was in Buffalo with the cousins. Ernie called out, "Damn it, Anne, wake up! Come on, open the door!" Ernie made such a racket, he woke up Papa.

The front porch light came on and Ernie ran to the door. It opened. Papa was standing there with a gun aimed at Ernie's head. Knowing full well Papa was absolutely capable of fulfilling his promise he frantically pleaded "No, no, please, no Papa, I promise, never again. Please, Papa, please!"

After hearing Ernie's pleas, Papa broke into hysterical laughter, dropping the gun. Ernie got away with a lot of shit, but Papa's anger was not to be taken lightly.

Cousin Sarah and Mom

Moms cousins and Buffalo Bills Daughters
Left to Right: Anne, Dad, Gloria, and Sarah (missing Rosie)

The Hustler

Ernie spent part of his youth in the local pool hall, fleecing all comers. A couple of old timers went to Papa to complain.

Spokesman: Don Paulo, your son comes to the pool hall and empties all the pockets.

Papa: Is my son a cheat?

Spokesman: No, no, Don Paulo, no.

Papa: If you don't want to lose, don't play him.

Ernie was the original Pin Ball Wizard. He could keep the ball in play and run the score to everyone's amazement.

When he was in prison he would sit at the Pac Man machine for hours just to fuck with the other prisoners who couldn't figure out how he could be so good. He had memorized the electronic pattern

The La Salle

Mama and Papa were in Florida and Papa took his car keys with him, meaning Ernie couldn't drive the car. So he walked into the LaSalle auto dealership. (LaSalle was part of the Cadillac division from 1927 through 1940.)

Everyone knew Ernie; he was Paul Palmeri's son. Ernie told them that his father lost his car keys, so the counterman made new keys. No charge. "My pleasure. My best to your father," said the counterman. "Yeah, sure, thank you," Ernie replied, with a smirk.

Ernie proceeded to smash the car and went back to the LaSalle dealership to get it fixed. In lieu of payment, Ernie promised to get his father to fix any problems they should have at the dealership. Knowing they would never ask for the favor.

Later, a friend of Papa's commented on the good job LaSalle did fixing his smashed automobile. "Ernie?" Papa asked, already knowing the answer.

The Little Guy

Ernie was cruising in his convertible with 3 other guys who were all slouching down. A car pulled up next to them, and the guys inside started harassing Ernie, thinking all the guys in Ernie's car were "little." Both cars emptied.

Surprise! The only little guy in the car was Ernie. Bigger surprise, "The Little Guy" (which became one of his aliases) threw the first punch. Short fight. Ernie and company got in their car and drove off, while the other guys just sat there looking beat and dismayed.

Ernie's Reputation

In Niagara Falls, while Papa was establishing himself as a man of respect amongst "the men of respect," Uncle Ernie was making his own name and establishing his reputation, in a good way. He had advanced intelligence and multiple talents: singer, comedian, natural born salesman, the kind of guy everyone wanted to be around.

Ernie would hire an orchestra and throw a big dance. He made money on tickets, program ads, food, etc. Everyone wanted in, the people who attended and the merchants who sponsored Paul Palmeri's son. Ernie always had ways to earn, one way or another.

Later, in the 1960s, Uncle Frank promoted some rock concerts and Ernie jumped in. They even had Frankie Valli and the Four Seasons.

The Fountain

Accident at the Fountain

In the 1940s, the Palmeris moved to New Jersey, WW2 was on, and Uncle Ernie, well, was Ernie. But for all his faults, Uncle Ernie had a warm and caring side. For example, the time he was out Christmas shopping and got rear-ended. He was right in front of the fountain across from Marrocco's Funeral Home.

Ernie jumped out of his car, screaming, "What's wrong with you? Where did you get your license?"

The man driving was visibly shaken and while not injured, still struggled to get out of the car, with tears in his eyes. He said "I'm sorry."

"You should be, look at my car," Ernie fumed.

The man kept sobbing, "I just found out my son was killed in the war."

This hit Ernie where it really hurt. Now Ernie is apologizing sympathetically "I'm sorry," he said. "Can I help you? Can I drive you someplace?"

"Please, take my name and number. I will pay for your damages," the man replied.

"Don't even think about it. Are you sure you're OK?" Ernie's compassion was sincere.

Cadillac Ernie

Uncle Ernie had a passion for Cadillacs, hence his nickname "Cadillac Ernie." In the fall of 1958, as was customary, the whole country waited anxiously for new car announcement day, but no one more than Cadillac Ernie. Ernie walked into Brogan Cadillac in Clifton, NJ. There was a 1959 yellow 2-door Caddy on the floor. The salesman approached, "Hi Ernie, beautiful, isn't it?"

"I'll take it," Ernie said. The salesman replied "I'm sorry Ernie," and explained that Ernie couldn't have it because Cadillac was on strike and they only had 3 cars (a demo, Mr. Brogan's and that one.) Ernie's response? "Pal, if you don't get this off the floor, you will be sorry."

When Ernie pulled up in his new Cadillac, all the neighborhood surrounded him. It was like that every year, 1960, '61, '62. One year, he got a convertible. Me and my cousins jumped into the car. The top was down, and water was hitting the windshield. Uncle Ernie told us it was raining. It took us a couple of seconds to realize the rain was only aimed at the windshield. The car had a windshield washer that sprayed water onto the glass.

The next year, we piled into the new Cadillac and he waved his hand in front of the radio and the station changed. We thought it was magical. Truth was there was a thin bar (called The Wonder Bar) under the carpet on the driver's side and when he tapped the bar, the radio changed stations. He loved gadgets as much as Cadillacs.

Uncle Ernie told me, "Never drive a Cadillac if you have to wash it yourself."

The Wire Room

When Dad was working for Willie Moretti in the wire room, Uncle Ernie would call Dad from the track and place a bet on the winner of a race just before it hit the wire.

One of Willie's guys caught on to what they were doing and told Willie, "Ernie's calling Joe and Joe's taking the bet before the results hit the wire."

"Pay 'em," Willie replied, nonchalantly. When Ernie came in to collect, the guy said to Ernie, "I told Willie what you and Joe are doing."

"What are you talking about?" Ernie took his payout and walked away, smiling.

Ernie was in his glory. He was in his late 20s, playing in the Organized Crime capital of the world, hanging with the who's who of OC, unlike Papa who stayed low key and presented himself as a retired undertaker.

One day, Joe Adonis walked into wire room. Dad was working and Ernie was hanging out. Joe A said to Ernie, "Let's take a ride."

They walked outside and Joe A tossed his car keys to Ernie. "You drive."

Joe Adonis, who was on the Board of Directors of The Commission, was known for his impeccable grooming. Ernie drove him to a haberdashery, and the staff was falling all over themselves to help Joe A, with Ernie watching and drooling.

Joe A told the shopkeeper to fit him for new shirts. Then he said to measure Ernie too, and give him a dozen "white on whites" (white shirt with white embroidery.)

"Go ahead, Ernie, pick out what you like, on me," said Joe A.

Ernie beamed. "Thank you, Joe."

The Luncheonette

Willie set up Uncle Ernie and Uncle Frank in a storefront taking action and put Giuseppe (Pepe) Sabato to watch over and handle any problems that might occur. Then he bought a luncheonette and relocated the operation. It was a low key spot. Willie spent time in the back booth, conducting. Ernie and Frank had to work the breakfast and lunch crowd. One lunch hour, this salesman walks in. Ernie and Frank were making sandwiches.

Salesman: Is the owner in?

Ernie: We're busy pal, its lunch time.

Salesman: I represent the premier linen service in town and want you to join our list of satisfied customers.

Ernie and Frank look at each other.

Ernie: Look pal, we have a linen service that we are happy with.

Salesman: You may want to reconsider. I work for Willie Moore's linen service.

Ernie and Frank look at each other.

Ernie: Frank, I'll be right back. Come with me, pal.

Ernie escorts the salesman to the back booth, where Willie was sitting.

Ernie: CUMP, this guy wants to sell us linen service. He says he works for you.

The salesman turns white, stuttering.

Salesman: I'm trying to make a living. I didn't mean any harm. I'm sorry.

Piss was running down his leg. Willy flicked his hand and the salesman left.

The Pink Elephant

There was this Italian restaurant called The Pink Elephant that served late night dinners. One night, Ernie, Dad and 2 other guys were sitting at table. Three Polacks were sitting at the bar, and this big dumb Polack says, "There a lot of greasy *guanines* in this place."

Ernie pushed the guy sitting next to him, to let him out of booth.

In unison, the guys said, "Calm down Ernie, come on Ernie."

But Ernie grabbed the loudmouth, spinning him off the stool, dropping him to his knees. Ernie put his gun in the Polack's mouth and the guy pissed himself. Tony Manzella came running out of kitchen, "No Ernie, please not here, no!"

Ernie said to the Polack's friends, "Get him out of here and don't let me see any of you anywhere. Get out!"

Going Legit

In 1950, during the Kefauver Hearings, Dad was splitting time between the wire room and driving Papa. Uncle Don was working in a liquor store to provide legitimacy. He was assigned the task and asked Dad to help him hide an arsenal, because search warrants were being issued.

After Willie Moretti died in October of 1951, the heat was still on. Things had to be different. Dad and most of their friends had legitimate jobs. Then Papa died in 1955 and things were really different.

Ernie and Frank got into the water softener business and were doing great. Their company, ABCO SALES, was making money and they were opening sales offices throughout New Jersey. Everybody was earning and it was legit.

Wayne, New Jersey

In the early 1960s, Uncle Ernie bought a new house in Wayne, NJ. One morning over coffee, Aunt Joan, who was usually calm, seemed agitated. Ernie asked her what was wrong and she told him she had a punch list of things that needed work. (Tiles popping off, door trim separating, paint issues and more.) While there was nothing major, she wanted everything fixed. After all this was a new house.

Ernie told her to call Henry, the contractor. She said she had called several times, but there was no answer. She left messages, with no response. There were several unfilled promises from Henry. Ernie told her he'd handle it.

So Ernie pulled up in his Caddy convertible and entered the construction trailer, approaching Henry, a fat guy with a cigar clenched between his teeth.

Henry: Hi Ernie.

Ernie: Forget the "hi," Henry. You've got Joan upset and when she is upset, I'm not happy.

Henry: OK Ernie.

Ernie: Now get your guys over to my house and fix whatever she wants.

Henry: OK Ernie.

Ernie: OK? What's OK?

Henry: Soon, Ernie, soon.

Ernie: Soon? What's soon? Now, Henry, now.

Ernie ripped the cigar out of Henry's mouth, pulled out his gun, put it under Henry's chin, and walked him out of the trailer. Henry, quaking and stammering, told his men, "Nobody leaves until Mrs. Palmeri says so."

After the work was completed, the house was perfect and Joan was happy, which made Ernie happy.

Ernie's Downfall

Mom always said if Ernie clicked, we were all set. Well, I guess you never know. Ernie got carried away with his power, which ultimately led to his downfall, as with most of these guys.

In the end, Ernie, who had made it and was on top of the world, turned his back on those people who were always there for him: his sister, his brother-in-law who he knew since they were babies, and me, the go-to for numerous, sometimes humorous escapades.

I did get his help one time there was a dock strike on and we couldn't get our Jaguars released. So I called him and told him the truth: I needed the cars to deliver 'cause I needed the money to stay afloat. Something Ernie understood all too well was "float." He made a call. I was allowed in, got the cars, and kept Camelot Motors open for a while.

Uncle Ernie and Mom on her wedding day

Uncle Ernie and Mom at Ernie's house in Florida

*Left to Right:
Uncle Ernie, Mom, and Papa*

Give a Man a Fish

Uncle Ernie's legacy for me was based on the proverb, "Give a man a fish and you feed him for a day; teach a man to fish and you feed him for a lifetime."

My personal proverb was modified to, "Give a man a fish and you feed him for a day; teach him to cheat, con, connive, scheme, and steal, and you feed him for a lifetime."

Uncle Frank

Uncle Frank, Mom's youngest brother, completed college and held a Bachelor's of Science degree. But the family influence has a powerful, magnetic pull.

Whatever was when Willie and Papa were alive, things were now different so both Frank and Ernie tried the legitimate route, as evidenced by their success in the water softener business.

Poly Clean

When the business slowed down to where they couldn't make it go, they both attempted other opportunities. One such opportunity was with an old college classmate of Uncle Frank's, Dr. Sol Sobal. Dr. Sobal had a brother, Nathan Sobal, who owned a chemical company, North American Chemical Co., in Patterson, NJ. Nathan was manufacturing detergent and cleaning products. One of the cleaners was a spray called "Poly Clean" which was an all-in-one like "Mr. Clean." Dr. Sobel confided in Frank that his brother needed to bring his sales to the next level.

Uncle Frank knew the influence of the Catenas had through the unions so he introduced Nathan to Jerry Catena, who turned him on to his brother Gene. Gene had Nathan hire his company, Best Sales, to get shelf space in all the supermarkets. As usual, everybody was making money.

Then some dummies, because they were being resisted by some store managers, decided to bomb a couple of A&Ps, and a store manager was killed. Typical Mob stupidity. They brought down so much heat; they killed the goose that laid the golden egg.

Uncle Frank took a job teaching science, dabbled in concert promotion, and eventually became extremely successful in the bathing suit manufacturing industry. He was the first to escape the stranglehold of our ancestry.

Unlike his brother Ernie, Frank always advised me to follow the right path and don't act like a Wise Guy. He was savvy to the times and realized the impact of guilt by association.

Frank Sinatra

In the 1960s, we were gathered at Uncle Frank's, after one of the concerts he promoted, when he said he'd like to get Frank Sinatra to do a concert.

While I knew of the association, I asked, "Why would he do a concert for you?"

"After what Marie's father did for him?" Uncle Frank replied. End of conversation.

It was years later, when I saw THE GODFATHER, with the now famous line, "He made him an offer he couldn't refuse," that I learned the details of how much Goombada Willie did for Ol' Blue Eyes.

Who Married Who

The press likes to make a fuss over people marrying into connected families. The truth is, in the 1920s through the 1950s, when families lived in the same neighborhoods, towns or areas, went to the same church, attended the same social functions, and were part of the same socioeconomic tier, what would you expect? Without E-Harmony.com they didn't have a lot of options.

Dad married Mom: the DiVitas and the Palmeris had been friends since Dad was two years old. Uncle Frank married Aunt Marie: Papa and Willie Moretti knew each other before Marie Moretti and Frank Palmeri were born. The same with Willie and Pete LaPlaca: Willie's daughter Rose married Pete's son Don. Anthony Bonasera married Joe DiCarlo's sister Sarah. And so on.

We were all schooled to marry Italian, but not one of the grandchildren complied!

My wife's grandparents were from Lebanon. The most interesting observation from our wedding day, on November 29, 1969, was how most of my family and friends could not relate to non-Italians in their innermost circle.

When Sandi and I were engaged, Aunt Marie told some people that her nephew was marrying a "lesbian." Of course everybody new she made a mistake, but really? Irish, French, German, and Polish, OK. But Lebanese?

Big Fight at Club 82

One night, in the late 1950's, Uncle Ernie took everyone out for the evening: Aunt Joan, Uncle Frank and Aunt Marie, Uncle Don and Aunt Rose, Mom and Dad, Mama and Aunt Marie (who was single at the time). They stopped into Club 82, a fag joint operated by Vito Genovese's wife.

They lined up a string of café tables and were watching the show. Three guys were sitting at a table near Mama.

Joan: Ernie change places with your mother.

Ernie: What's up Joan?

Joan: Just change places.

Ernie: Mama, change places.

This drunk that Aunt Joan noticed bothering Mama grabbed Mama's hand, and said "where you going", so Ernie grabbed his hand and cold-cocked him. Mayhem ensued, tables flying.

Joey Giardello (the middleweight champion) tackled Uncle Don. Aunt Rose started beating on Joey with her glass pocketbook.

While Joey was trying to hold Uncle Don down and defend against Aunt Rose, he yelled, "Rose, please, I'm trying to keep Donnie from killing somebody."

Meanwhile, female impersonators were on stage doing a show, singing "Rose of Washington Square."

Lou Lou

Our motto was, "I can get it for you wholesale."

Louis DiVita and Paul Palmeri

My name is Louis Paul DiVita. I have been known as "Louis Paul," "LPD," "Big Lou," "Cousin Lou, "Louie," and, as I've aged, "Uncle Lou." After a wrong way-run in with a knife, I was "Louie the Blade." But my favorite was Mama's name for me, "Lou Lou."

There were other people named Louis in my family. Of course, my grandfather and uncle (Dad's father and brother). But in my generation, there's Uncle Louis' son Louis, who died from nephritis at the age of twelve. And don't forget my older brother Louis and Aunt Marie's baby named Louis, both buried in the family plot. An irony was that, Papa was preceded by two brothers named Paolo. Paulo #1 died at the age of 7 in 1890, Paulo #2 died at 2 months old 1891.

My younger sister Anne was named after Mom. My younger brother Joe was named after Dad. Uncle Ernie's son "Big Paul" and Uncle Frank's son "Little Paul" were named after Papa. Uncle Ernie's daughter Elena and Frank's daughter Elena were named after Mama. Cousin Ernie is named after his dad and Mama's father, etc. Carrying on family names was the norm, certainly for Italians.

Macy's Thanksgiving Parade

I was probably four or five years old when Dad put me in the car and we went to pick up Papa. We were headed to New York to see the parade. I was sitting on the armrest between Dad and Papa. I don't think they had child safety seats and I know there were no seat belts.

As we rode through the Lincoln tunnel, the humming of the tires, the wishing sounds echoing off the tiles and the glass booths where the Transit cops are stationed were all part of the experience. Whenever we went through the tunnel the adults had to make a point that we were under the river. I couldn't wait to see daylight. Anyway as we emerged the excitement mounted. I was going to attend something I had previously seen on TV.

We moved through the city and after Dad parked, we walked a short distance and went into a huge apartment building and took the elevator up to a beautiful apartment. When we entered, the man and his wife escorted me to an open window where I perched for my bird's-eye view.

Although the weather was brisk the sun was shining bright and I felt like I could touch the balloons. I have made my brain ache trying to remember whose place it was and I can't, but I know he was one of THE BOYS

A WISER GUY

There were people who I remember as more acquaintances than close friends, but, at the time, they were all just "Papa's friends."

Rockefeller Center Tree

I remember around 1953-54 (I was 5 or 6) when Uncle Ernie and Dad took me to New York City to pick up Grandma DeDe (Dad's mom) at Grand Central station. We were early, so Ernie said we should go to see the tree at Rockefeller Center. We got there at about 10 PM and were the only ones there.

All I wanted was one of the ornaments and Ernie hung over the rail like he was picking fruit, trying to get one for me. He couldn't reach the ornaments, of course, but I was grateful he tried. Later, we picked up Grandma DeDe and she got off the train carrying her standard bakery box with her famous cannoli shells.

In 2007, we went to New Jersey to spend Christmas with my brother Joe and his family. We arrived on December 23rd and went out for dinner. When we emerged from the restaurant, Joe had arranged for a limo, and off we went to see the tree, my wife Sandi's favorite NYC site at Christmas.

Over the years, on most visits to NYC and the famous tree, I would drop Sandi off and circle in the car because there was no parking. That day, the limo dropped us off 4 to 5 blocks away and we had to walk in. The crowd was 10 deep from the rail — vastly different from my visit 50 plus years earlier.

The Bike Accident

In 1957, Dad bought me a new bike for my ninth birthday. A few weeks later, I was going to the park with my friends when I decided to challenge an oncoming car. The car won.

I had a compound fracture of my left wrist, broken a right arm and numerous cuts, scrapes and contusions. I spent a week in the hospital and 3 months in hard casts. Great summer. No air conditioning, of course. I couldn't play much, so I was stuck inside. Aunt Marie spent her vacation taking me places to break the monotony.

Uncle Ernie wanted to go after the woman who hit me but everybody talked him out of it. She was shaken up, but put me in the car and drove me to the hospital.

Of course we sued. And the lawyers prepped me to say what they wanted me to say. I did exactly what I was told and ended up with $7,000. It was my first performance. And it set the precedent for me. If you are prepared, stick to your story, don't let anybody rattle you, and you can win.

Fair Lawn

In 1958, Dad decided to buy a house in Fair Lawn, NJ, three houses from Uncle Ernie.

Growing up, I spent a lot of time with Uncle Ernie and my cousins, who were closer in age to me than my brother and sister. At one time we were inseparable as a family, all the aunts, uncles, and cousins. Unfortunately, success, failure, kids and grandkids drove a wedge into our closeness and what once seemed to be eternal.

One Sunday, we were out for a ride. Yes, believe it or not in the 1950s, 60s and 70s, families ventured out for a Sunday leisurely ride, which included stopping for an ice cream cone, or a Texas wiener, or sometimes both. A Texas wiener is indigenous to New Jersey. It is a hot dog with chilly and onions. Of course, there was always a fight as to where to go. Like the famous Pat's and Gino's cheesesteak war in Philly; we had the Texas wiener wars in Jersey: The Hot Grill, Falls View, Pappy's, Callahan's, Johnny and Hanges, etc.

For all his faults, Ernie had a warm and caring side. On one particular Sunday, we came across a house on fire. Ernie stopped the car, rushed into the house and helped the people save their belongings.

My Friend Vinnie

When I was in the fifth grade, I had a fight with Vinnie Galasso in the school cafeteria. We got suspended from the cafeteria and had to walk home for lunch. Seeing as we lived 2 blocks from each other, we became friends, and our parents became friends, and we spent a lot of time with each other's families. We became so close that my brother Joe asked Mr. G to be his confirmation sponsor.

One Sunday morning, Vinnie called. They were going to the Mets game, did I want to go? Of course I did. Mr. G picked me up and off we went. Mr. G was a visionary. We had a bag filled with eggplant parm sandwiches, long before you were banned from bringing stuff into the stadium and they had gourmet concessions.

Mr. G invited Mom and Dad to a dinner dance in their old neighborhood in Brooklyn. Mr. G's brother Nick ran the Democrat Club, and they were having their annual fundraiser. People were dancing, eating, drinking, and having a good time. A figure approached, and Dad jumped up to acknowledge him. It was Sonny Franzese.

Mr. G tugged on Dad's jacket to sit down. "Joe what are you doing? You know who he is? You can't just stop a man like him."

Nobody really knew where we came from, and Dad had to give Mr. G a briefing as to why it was OK to greet Sonny. He gave him a short overview without going into detail.

See, a lot of people want to be OK with mobsters, but at arm's length. And when a hoodlum gets pinched, they want distance. So for us and the times we were living in, there was no sense talking about the past.

My Other Cousin

Uncle Ernie told me as a boy nothing thrilled him more than watching Papa get dressed and put on his gun.

When I was twelve years old, I bought my first barbell set. I was in the basement lifting weights when Uncle Ernie came downstairs and asked me what I was doing.

"I'm lifting weights. I want to be big and strong so I can take care of myself," I said proudly.

Ernie opened his jacket, revealing his holstered 38.

"My little nephew, when you have your COUSIN with you, the biggest men will cringe," He said. As I aged that statement became a reality.

I couldn't wait to get my first gun and stand in front of the mirror and admire how I looked. With the excitement I felt, and now I fully understood what he was teaching me.

I acquired my first gun while I was someplace I wasn't supposed to be; subsequently, I purchased numerous guns for myself and for resale in the street. I knew the people I sold to were not crazies, and that while the guns were not going to be used for sport they also would not be used for senseless assaults and/or killings.

I'm almost embarrassed to admit to these purchases and sales because today I am a staunch advocate for closing gun show loop holes, extensive back ground checks and a ban on assault weapons

Learning to Shoot

During the summers following Mr. Volpe's death in 1958, I spent time with his daughter Angela and son-in-law Ettore Agolino and their family. I always marveled how attached Ettore was to the elders, as they would sit in the backyard in straight backed chairs from the kitchen and dining room, telling stories and drinking homemade wine with fruit, usually peaches. Sometimes Ettore would bring out his guitar and they would sing Sicilian songs.

Ettore would tell stories about Papa with almost a sacred reverence. Ettore was an attorney and represented Russell Bufalino. Ettore's brother-in-law, Charles Bufalino, was married to Tina Volpe, and was also an attorney. They lived next door to the Agolino family. Charlie's brother, William Bufalino, was the attorney for the Teamsters and Jimmy Hoffa.

Charlie owned acreage with a small lake and had a railroad caboose converted to a cabin where he stayed when he went hunting. He was an avid hunter and marksman. He had an amazing gun collection. In his collection, he had pistols custom made for his grip and aim.

I was mesmerized by his variety of firearms and it fostered my affection for guns. Charlie taught me how to shoot. His intent was strictly for sport. Unlike Uncle Ernie.

Crazy Stunts

One summer. Uncle Ernie invited me to a painting party. Aunt Joan had gone to Niagara Falls with the younger kids, but Uncle Ernie, Paul and Little Ernie were home. My cousin Elena was at work, as a beautician.

It was one of the hottest summers I ever experienced. We had one fan to be shared by all of us. At night, Ernie would take the fan into his bedroom, leave the door open, and tell us we would benefit from the "fruits of cross ventilation." We were miserable. Cross Ventilation, My Ass.

The fridge was broken, we had nothing to eat. "Stop your whining," Ernie said, "when we get finished, we will get something to eat."

When Elena came home from work, Ernie asked her if she got paid. She said yes, so he asked her how much. "Two hundred and fifteen dollars," she said.

"Everybody get dressed, we're going out," Ernie said. "Elena, give me the money." We all thought we were going for a burger or something, so we piled into the car.

We pulled up to Donahue's, a fine dining restaurant. We walked in like we owned the place and proceeded to order duck dinners all around.

Then Ernie tells the waiter he forgot his Diners Club card, and the waiter immediately offers to open a house charge. We ate for free. And Ernie had the $200.

In later years, Ernie said many times he could never pull off some of his stunts now. How true.

Wanna Buy a Duck?

In 1950, when the Senate Committee questioned America's most recognized mobsters, among them was Goombada Willie, who talked about his house in Deal, New Jersey. When asked about his Deal house, he testified he bought the house from the Lincoln National Bank of Newark, New Jersey. The house was in foreclosure and taxes were due.

A little known fact, the house had been owned by comedian Joe Penner, who had a catch phrase, "Wanna Buy a Duck?" Goombada Willie raised ducks on the grounds. Years later, the fictitious Tony Soprano raised ducks. "Mob Wife" Lynda Milito said her husband Louie raised ducks.

Once again, we were so irreverent we went to Donahue's and ordered ducks all around.

Earning

I was always the good kid. Whenever anyone needed help, call Louis. I was strong, capable, and had a burning desire to please everyone, but I always looked, listened and learned.

My cousin Big Paul (Ernie's son) and myself were altar boys and volunteered to serve the 6 AM mass. Because if we served the 6 o'clock mass we got the funerals, which got you out of school, and also the weddings on weekends. Either way, we got paid $10 per man. In 1958-59 that was big.

I always earned: Christmas cards, paper route, cut grass, wash and wax cars, and whatever Uncle Ernie threw my way.

After the water softener business tanked, Uncle Ernie took over Carm's, a charcoal restaurant in Totowa, NJ. I would take 2 buses to go help out. He had other things going on, but I was not privy. Then he took over a big place called the Western Charcoal Pit, a highway location attached to a bowling alley.

When that failed, Ernie did a move which backfired and he fled to Florida. Oh well, things happen.

I Can Get It for You Wholesale.

When Ernie had the restaurants, he was also taking action. He taught me how to shoplift. At about 11 or 12 years old, believe me, I was far from innocent. I was the pretzel monitor in the first through fourth grade and handled the cash. I had a big round tin of pretzels and sold them for 2 cents apiece at recess. I always took my cut. I also collected for the hot dog lunches and crumb cake and hot chocolate breakfast fundraisers. Would you believe at the age of 7 I was skimming? It's in our blood.

Ernie took pilferage to a new level. Our motto was, "I can get it for you wholesale." He for some reason was drawn to Two Guys from Harrison, founded in Harrison, New Jersey. In 1959 they opened additional locations and the name was shortened to "Two Guys." They were the precursor of Walmart, Target etc. Not that he cared, but Two Guys was making plenty so they could afford him as a silent partner! While we used the store on Rt 4 in Fair Lawn, he made the Rt 46 Totowa location his number one warehouse.

He took orders: toiletries, small appliances, meat, etc.

I was initially a lookout. When someone was approaching the aisle he was working I would call out to him like, "hey Uncle Ernie," to tip him off and he would just start browsing or pushing the cart till he got to an empty aisle.

We would pick out the items he had orders for, then he would find an empty aisle and load the bags with high-priced items like meat, toiletries, small appliances etc. He would stack open bags in the cart and then top the bag with cereal boxes, detergent, and his favorite, paper towels. When he went through the checkout, he had already bagged everything and he would tell the cashier in the bags was 4 rolls of paper towels, 4 boxes of Cheerios or whatever. Meanwhile the bags were filled with high priced items. The cashiers loved him because in those days there were no scanners and the cashier had to pound out every key and total each item and then bag them.

He was so thoughtful; all they had to do was ring towels, detergent, cereal or whatever he told them was in the bags. To insure the cashiers' cooperation, every now and then he would pull out a couple of packages of ground beef or stew meat from under the paper towels, which had to be on top so as to not to get crushed, and read off the price tags declaring value so as not to arouse suspicion.

Another technique was to buy towels, cereal etc. Pay, get to the door and say he forgot something. Meanwhile I was in the store loading another cart while he was checking out. Then he would put back some of the bulk items. He would load the bags with the meat and, after the bags were reloaded, he would stand by with his cart and his receipt while I went through the checkout and paid for a six pack of coke or a couple of cans of tomatoes. Then we would walk out together.

The security guards were stationed in front of the store, clueless. There were no cameras and I don't recall convex mirrors, all contributing to our success. Considering today's cyber-crime, we were primitive but effective.

Then he organized the security guards and warehousemen and, once he had the delivery guys on board, large appliances were on the menu. We all worked together. One time Ernie walked out carrying an entire swing set, waving at the security guards.

Englewood Golf and Country Club

I couldn't count on the few bucks that came my way. I wanted my own money. So Uncle Don got me a job at The Englewood Golf and Country Club, working for Jerry Volpe, the club owner and golf pro. I was there about three years, between the ages of 13 and 16.

Englewood's membership was made up of a who's who of celebrities, show business people, ball players and Wise Guys. Everyone from athlete Althea Gibson, to entertainer Corbet Monica, to high ranking teamster official Tony Pro.

Comedian Joey Bishop would give me an envelope with the script for his sitcom ("The Joey Bishop Show" with Abbey Dalton) and I would read it between my duties. Anthony Scotto, the head of the ILA union, was a member. Frank Erickson would tip me $5 to put his and his friend Juniata's clubs in their trunk. Mr. Erickson was the bookmaker's bookmaker, and wasn't leaving anything of his anywhere out of his control.

I would bring out the golf bags for the members and put them on the railing till the caddies picked them up. When they came back, I had to wipe down the clubs; clean the faces, wipe the bag, and put them in the slots. They taught me how to re-grip clubs. I was in charge of the balls for the driving range, collected the money and, as a bonus, Jerry let me keep the money.

One Saturday morning it was raining. I had to take two buses to get to Englewood, hoping the weather would clear so I could make a day's pay. We had no cell phones in 1962 to find out what was going on.

Jerry said the club was going to be closed, but if the weather cleared, some of his friends were coming up, and if I wanted to hang around I could caddy. I had free run of the kitchen, so I figured what the hell.

Well, the weather broke, and I caddied for Jerry, Buddy Hackett, Rocky Graziano and Ralph Terry. Terry was playing in the World Series at the time. They played 5 or 6 holes. I had so many laughs, I would have carried for free. Of course, they all tipped well.

Ralph Terry asked me if I liked baseball. Of course I did. He told me to write down my name and there would be two World Series tickets for Tuesday's game (which was played on Wednesday because of rain on Tuesday.) Terry was pitching. I had a dilemma. See, he was pitching against the Giants and me and Dad were Giant fans. Ralph Terry was the winning pitcher.

Tony Bender

Our old friend and perennial watch dog Giussppe (Pepe) Sabato was now watching the Englewood Golf and Country Club for Thomas (Tommy Ryan) Eboli, acting boss of the Genovese family. A big step up from watching out for Uncle Ernie and Frank's bookmaking operation.

Later, when I was in my 20s and Dad felt it was old news, he told me about one morning at the club in April 1962. Dad was sitting in the grill room with Pep when they noticed Anthony (Tony Bender) Strollo walk onto the putting green. Tony Bender was always well dressed and impeccably groomed, but this morning he was disheveled.

Pep jumped up and went outside to the green. As Pep approached him, shrugging his shoulders, Tony Bender's hands were flailing and his voice was loud, but Dad couldn't hear what was being said. Besides, Dad got up and went to the men's room, so when Pep came back, it didn't look like he had been watching. Sometimes it's best to make yourself scarce.

Pep was probably 20 years younger than Papa and his contemporaries, but he was old school. Nobody knew how powerful Pepe Sabato became, but Tony Bender going to see Pep at the club apparently pleading for his life, right before he disappeared. It makes you wonder.

Pep was still active in 1991, when I left New Jersey, and if my calculations are right he was 83.

Ed Sullivan

Jerry Volpe sold his interest in the club and retired as pro. The new owners hired a good old boy pro, Glen Teal. He asked Dad if I would be interested in working for him, so I did. He was a real pain in the ass, obviously did not understand where I come from, but it was not worth telling Pep.

Ed Sullivan was a regular at the club. He would take a cart and caddy, shoot a few holes, come back, go to the grill room, have a sandwich and iced tea, and leave. One morning, Mr. Sullivan walked into the pro shop. Glen Teal tried to suck up. "Hello Mr. Sullivan, I'm Glen Teal, the club pro. This is my wife Rhoda, and my assistant pro, Bob LaBelle."

Ed Sullivan saw me standing in the doorway between the pro shop and the bag room. He walked up to me, extended his hand and said, "You must be the other assistant pro, I'm Ed Sullivan." I shook his hand and said, "I'm Lou DiVita, nice to meet you."

I felt like a million bucks. And there stood the three stooges.

Bob LaBelle did not like me and he had a caddy he wanted to give my job to. (I think he may have been a chicken hawk.) Anyway, he was fucking with me, so I grabbed an iron and assured him I would split his head open. So I was fired.

A WISER GUY

When Pep asked me what happened, I told him we had a misunderstanding and I handled it. So he put me in the locker room, shining shoes. I had a buffing wheel and the locker man would bring me the street shoes. I would polish them, and after the round, I would clean and polish the golf spikes. I would do 300 pair per day, Saturday and Sunday.

Bernie Brillstein

One Saturday morning, Bernie Brillstein came into my room. He was a young William Morris talent agent who went on to be a famous manager and producer (THE SOPORANOS was his).

BB: Good morning, Lou.

Lou: Good morning, Mr. Brillstein.

BB: Lou, I have an important engagement tonight, make them shine.

Lou: Sure thing, Mr. Brillstein.

So I put my all into shining those shoes. Later that afternoon…

Lou: Here you go Mr. Brillstein.

BB: Wow, they look like patent leather. I knew I could count on you.

He reached in his pocket and handed me a fin.

Lou: Thank you, Mr. Brillstein.

BB: Thank you, Lou.

Lou: Anytime.

I was excited because he was so happy, and the finsky didn't hurt either. Tommy the locker man came in and asked me what that was all about, so I told him.

"Mr. Brillstein brought me a pair of shoes this morning and asked me to give them special care, so I made them look like glass and he was so happy he gave me a five dollar tip."

I was being paid $15 cash a day. That night, Tommy shorted my pay $5. So I told my father and Sunday morning, when I came into work, Tommy gave me five bucks and said, "Hey sorry, I made a mistake on your pay last night. (Mistake MY ASS!)

But I said "Thanks, Tommy," As I glanced up, I saw Pep looking in.

School

I graduated the 8th grade at St. Ann's in Fair Lawn and had been accepted to one of the Catholic high schools, but I decided to go to public school: Memorial Junior High for the ninth grade and then onto Fair Lawn High School.

I had a lot of difficulty in school, primarily because I didn't care. The teachers were constantly harping to my parents that I had a high IQ but did not apply myself. Today, I'd probably be diagnosed with ADD. If I liked something, I couldn't get enough. If I didn't like something, you couldn't jam it down my throat.

Louis The Hairdresser

I was always planning my future and basically wanted to earn. The question was, how? I got the idea to be a hairdresser. So I stopped going to school and hung out at Broadway Barber Shop, owned by Frank Ceilo.

Like a lot of my friends my first car was a Junker, a 1953 Pontiac convertible that needed everything, but it ran. I am a mechanically inept individual, but even I was able to do the ongoing fixes that were required of $50 cars.

One afternoon a friend of Frank's, a guy named Bobby who was also a barber, came flying through the front door of the shop. He was in a state of panic because he needed $125 to pay his bookmaker.

Three weeks earlier, he had bought a 1957 Oldsmobile Delta 88 four door, hard top, white, with a red interior and a J2 engine (the engine had three 2Barrel carburetors). It was a real sleeper in pristine condition for $500. He got the car from an elderly couple he knew and wanted him to get this great deal after they were no longer able to drive.

He was so scared there had to be more to the story, but I didn't care. I went in the back and called Dad and asked for a loan to buy the car. Dad told me where to find the money and emphasized to take only $125. Bobby drove me to my house where I paid him and got one of the best deals I ever made. There is a lot of truth in the adage "Being in the right place at the right time"

When I got caught cutting school, Dad found out and was pissed. There were lots of fights, but he finally gave in and let me quit high school. Mama tried to be encouraging, but Mom was heartbroken. Being a high school dropout was not in her plans for me. They all hoped that I would rise above, somehow, someway.

Dad had an acquaintance, Mike, who owned Michele of Paris, a big New York salon. Dad took me to meet him, and Mike said to be a good stylist I had to cut hair to the style, which I would not learn in a regular beauty school.

So my first step was when Dad enrolled me in Atlas Barber School at 42nd and Broadway, where they taught theory. Then it was down to 13th Street to work on the bowery bums. Face it, no sober man is going to let kids with shaky hands shave them or cut their hair.

In 1964-65, when I was at the Atlas Barber School, men's hair styling became in vogue, primarily due to the celebrity of Hollywood stylist Jay Sebring, whose life was cut short by Charlie Manson in 1969.

When I got my certificate, I had to apprentice and Uncle Ernie put me with Carmelo Santora, in Garfield, NJ. I knew Mello since I was a kid. He had me sweeping, cleaning mirrors and windows, running for coffee, etc. When people came in Monday through Thursday, I had to tell them to come back later 'cause Mello was in the back taking action or playing cards.

It only took me a month to figure out this was not for me. Broadway Barbers was closed, so I started hanging out at Charlie's

Barber Shop, also in Fair Lawn, where I helped out and actually got to cut hair when the shop was busy. At Charlie's, I met and started collecting for a couple of bookmakers. But again, I realized I was in a dead end. I was earning, but no future.

Beating The System

I went to Fair Lawn High School and looked up my old guidance counselor, Mrs. Harrison. She was happy to see me and said if I went to summer school, took English and history (which were two of my best subjects) and then took extra classes during the school year, she would get me out with my class. The Class of 1966. I was doing well, finally living up to my potential, getting all grades in the 90s (out of 100).

So, as a high school dropout, I actually graduated in 3 years instead of 4. I beat the system!

Around March of '66, Mrs. Harrison summoned me to her office. Mr. Riley, the Vice Principal, who had it in for me, pointed out the school required all students to take "Typing 10," a class usually completed in the 10th grade. This class was required for graduation. It was too be later for me to take it at school, so Mrs. Harrison enrolled me in the Ridgewood Secretarial School, nights. Me and 30 chicks. Who better than me? Well, I got through, but I still can't type.

The night of my graduation, I passed Mr. Riley in the hall, and held out my diploma with a big grin.

"That diploma was printed with disappearing ink," Mr. Riley quipped.

"Fuck you," I promptly replied.

Accomplishments

During that year, I not only got good grades, but I organized a successful toy drive for an orphanage, collecting more toys than ever before, and throwing a party like they had never seen.

I also petitioned the school board to allocate an empty lot owned by the school, to be an outdoor student lounge, where smoking would be permitted. (Before the Surgeon General informed us smoking was hazardous to our health.) There had been complaints to the school and calls to the police from nearby homeowners, who didn't want crowds of kids congregating in front of their houses, smoking and making noise. I thought I came up with a great solution, so did the school board.

From Cutting Hair To Cutting Grass

While Uncle Ernie was in exile in Florida, I started at Rockland Community College, where I attended for two years. No AA degree, just credits.

While attending RCC, I was pumping gas at a station in Monsey, NY. A customer told me if I wanted to earn, I should get some lawn mowers. People were clamoring for lawn cutters.

So I went to Chris & Buds, a local lawnmower shop, and made a deal with the owners for equipment on credit. I bought a truck and was in business.

Dad came home, saw the truck in front of the house with all the equipment on it, and asked what this was all about. When I explained, he was flabbergasted that I was able to pull it off. It was one of his proudest moments, and was one of his favorite Louis stories.

"Mr. Lawn" did well for two years. Then Ernie returned and I let the business go because I was going to be with him.

My First Collection

While Ernie was on sabbatical, I was collecting for the bookmakers that I had met at the barber shop. My posture, knowledge, and education all helped my reputation for being able to handle any situation. And I was doing it on my own merits.

My first collection was in a lower middle class neighborhood. The stiff was a factory worker. I was with a guy named Charlie, who was non-assuming. My presence was to send a message.

We stood on the porch, Charlie knocked, and this deadbeat opens the door. I remember cooking smells from the kitchen, kids running up to see what's going on, and a baby crying.

Deadbeat: Hey.
Charlie: Whata you got?
Deadbeat: Charlie, I need time.
Charlie: You know how this thing works. Step outside.
Deadbeat: Please Charlie, there's no overtime. They're trying to repo my car. I gotta get groceries.
Charlie: Empty your pockets.
The guy turns his pockets inside out. Charlie counts out $155.
Charlie: You're short. We'll be back tomorrow.
Deadbeat: I got no place to go.

Charlie: Tomorrow.

We walked away and got into the car. On the porch, I stood in there. But when we got in the car, Charlie saw I was tight.

Charlie said, "Listen to me, kid. If we didn't take the money, he would have bet it with someone else, trying to win the car payment or groceries."

From that day forward, I had no feelings when I was collecting.

Ernie's Return

When Ernie was feeling some heat, he moved to Florida, of all places. Later when the climate cooled up north, he made his way back to New Jersey. On his return from exile, the first thing he called me for was to pick him up in Hawthorne, NJ.

My mother woke me, "Your uncle called. He said hurry up, pick him up at this gas station."

When I got there, he was nowhere to be found so I got out of my car and looked around. Here comes Ernie with Ron. Ron was married to my cousin Elena. I knew him since I was 12 and he was 16.

"Come on, we have to go," yelled Ernie.

We all jumped in the car. I had a single key and it was stuck in the bottom of my jeans pocket. Ernie's yelling, Ron is laughing, and I'm struggling.

We finally got out of there, but I never lived down how I screwed up the getaway.

Turns out, Ernie had commandeered two trucks and trailers in Florida, but courteously returned them to an agency in New Jersey.

Riding With Ernie

Ernie was back in town and he wanted me with him. Mostly, I rode around with him. Sometimes I waited in the car, sometimes I accompanied him. Sometimes I'd sit with him, sometimes I'd sit by myself or just wait. Sometimes he tells me what's going on, other times he's mum.

Then sometimes he'd call and say, "Dress up, Lou, we're going to New York."

Once we went to Vesuvius, a famous Italian restaurant in mid-town. We walked to the rear, passing other tables to talk to Russell Bufalino. (Russ had taken over from Santo Volpe and Joe Barbara.) Russ's wife Carolyn and Mom knew each other since childhood, and would visit at least once a year. Russ knew me from the day I was born, but hadn't seen me in several years.

"Russ, you remember Anne's boy Louis," Ernie said. Russ introduced me to the other men at the table. First names only, but I knew Johnny Dio from his pictures. Ernie ordered me to sit at a table (out of ear shot) and told me to order whatever I wanted. Johnny Dio suggested he order for me.

I had been eyeing a magnificent platter of macaroni, the likes I had never seen. My plate was a little smaller. As big as I was, I guess they didn't think I could eat the whole platter. But the linguine Carbonara was the best dish of macaroni I ever had. It's still one of my favorites, never been able to duplicate it. Sometimes I think it was the whole experience. We made several trips back there and whatever we ate, I had to have at least a Carbonara appetizer.

Ol'Blue Eyes

As usual, I got my nightly call from Uncle Ernie. "I'm going in. I'm taking Ernie and Linda; they want to see ROSEMARY'S BABY. If you want to come, OK, but I don't need you," he said.

So I casually replied, "You know what, I'm gonna pass. Haven't seen my friends in a week. Thanks, talk to ya."

I don't know if I proved to be a dumb-ass or just unlucky. After the movie, Uncle Ernie took Linda and Little Ernie to Jilly's for a drink. And, oh yeah, he was there!

They no sooner walked in the door when Frank Sinatra bolts toward Ernie. Because Ernie and Frank Sinatra knew each other from the Hasbrouck Heights days. And because, you know, Goombada Willie made an offer Tommy Dorsey couldn't refuse.

I wasn't there that night, but I heard about it:

Frank: Ernie, I haven't seen you in years, how you doin'?
Ernie: OK Frank, you know me.
Frank: You look great!
Ernie: Frank this is my son Ernie, and my daughter Linda.
Frank: Let's have a drink.

The moral of the story? I didn't get to meet Sinatra.

Back When I Was Rich And Famous

Who was better than me?

Big Plans

It was early 1967 when Pete LaPlaca was released from prison. He was visited by his nephew Peter (Pete Cass) Castiglia, who was a street banker. Pete Cass asked his uncle to intervene on Ernie's behalf, so that Ernie could return to New Jersey from Florida.

Upon Ernie's return, we immediately started spending a lot of time together. And, as usual, Ernie had big plans. Shortly thereafter, Ernie started doing things for Pete LaPlaca, and Mom told me to make myself scarce. Pete was under constant surveillance.

Then in 1968, Pete LaPlaca's right hand guy, Danny Polidori, died suddenly of a heart attack. Pete was in a conundrum. He needed someone who knew most, if not all of the players and powers. Who better than Ernie?

I made a few trips to Pete's house, but that stopped. Because Mom didn't want me to be around, and because one of Pete's granddaughters liked me, but the feelings weren't mutual. At that point I wasn't welcome. Oh, well.

Uncle Ernie ("The Little Guy") went on to become huge. Pete LaPlaca placed Ernie as the business agent at Teamsters Local 945. He controlled the waste industry in New Jersey. Nothing happened in garbage without his blessing.

Unfortunately, he got a little too big and had a problem with the Federal Government concerning banks and pension funds.

Who's Sorry Now?

On March 6, 1981, Attorney George A. Franconero was found by his wife face down in the snow, lying next to his car. George, the brother of singer Connie Francis, was taking a permanent nap.

As I have mentioned, everybody wants to be close to The Boys until the climate warms, then they try to distance themselves. George supposedly worked in concert with Uncle Ernie introducing him to bankers and assisting him to obtain fraudulent loans and kickbacks for officials of Local 945 of the Teamsters' Union, which was often referred to as "The Crown Jewel of the Genovese Crime Family."

The assassination took place following Uncle Ernie's unsuccessful appeal, making him the number one suspect. The good news was, George's testimony implicated others before and during his association with Uncle Ernie, and he was due to testify in several upcoming mob trials.

So when it comes to who did it? It's a "pick 'em."

Rogers Peet

In 1968, when I was 20, I took a part time job selling high-end men's furnishings at Rogers Peet, which was a respected, long-established New York City men's store. Quickly, I realized the real earning potential and set up my own "I can get it for you wholesale" business.

I was taking orders, like we did at "TWO GUYS from HARRISON." I had them wrapped for shipping, then the shipping and receiving manager would drop them at my house. It was all mine. I didn't have to share or get paid corks for my labor. That was my eye opener and set my future path.

While I was working there, a large man named Marty Weiner came in. I couldn't fit him and told him I would special order his shirts. Marty was impressed with the way I handled myself and asked me if I ever thought about selling cars. He invited me to see him on my day off and meet his partner, Manny Sicari. Marty and Manny owned "Ken Rambler" in Paramus, New Jersey.

The other salesman at their dealership was "Big Jim," who had a lucrative career as a jewel thief and second story man. See, in the 1950s and '60s, a large number of con artists, thieves and bandits gravitated to the car business. Why not? Free car, gas, a desk and telephone, and an opportunity to earn.

Sandi

While I was working at Rogers Pete, the guys I worked with told me I had to see the girl that managed the Russell Stover store in the mall. They were right. She was beautiful, intelligent and personable. We started dating and were married eleven months later and have been married for 46 years.

In retrospect, while the wedding was great and one of my happiest days (along with our daughter Jennifer's birth), there was some controversy. Sandi's father was an extremely successful engineer and president of an international consulting, engineering and construction company. His friends were all successful professionals who dressed conservatively in dark suits that were considered proper attire for the occasion.

And then there was my side that, shall we say, they added color? But that's a story in and of itself for another time.

Camelot

So my connections at the men's store led to my first job as a car salesman. My first week in the car business (February 1969) netted $500 plus paycheck, a new demo to drive, gas and benefits. Who's better than me? The best part? I had a whole new outlet for any merchandise I came across. I knew guys who ran other businesses from the dealerships. Myself, I sold discount merchandise: stereos, car stereos, labeled clothing, etc. Things that the buyers believed was swag.

Uncle Ernie said he could get me a factory job from the union, salting and seeding, for the hourly pay, plus money from the union totaling about $300 a week. And for all this glory, I risked getting a pipe wrench to my skull. But if I did a good job recruiting and survived, I might get to be a business agent. No thanks.

Shortly after I was hired at Ken Rambler, Marty and Manny split. Marty went to Florida and bought a dealership in Pompano. Manny changed the name of the dealership to Rallye Motors.

I got very close to Manny over the next few years. Fiat had a sales contest and I won a trip to Italy. Sandi and myself went with Manny and his wife Joan. Joan was the reason he had the dealership; it was her father's and she took it as part of her inheritance. While on the trip, I bonded with Bernie Treich, who approached me a few months later to partner with him. Leon Feldstein, the owner of Camelot Motors in Bergenfield, New Jersey, was looking to sell.

Camelot Motors sold Fiat, Austin and MG. I went to work for Leon for a few months, and then we bought him out. Bernie held 60%, I held 40%, but we cut it up 50/50.

Leon Feldstein was a very interesting man. He was in a concentration camp, in his teens and after he was liberated, he was part of the Exodus. He survived in the camp because he was mechanically inclined. The SS lined up the boys and went down the line asking if they had a skill. The boy next to Leon said, "Tell them you're a mechanic." When the SS officer asked Leon his skill, he replied, "mechanic." The officer swiftly put a gun to Leon's head and said if he lied he was dead. As Leon said, God was with him. He was able to do the assigned repair. Leon survived the ordeal by making cigarette lighters for the SS from scrap metal. One lighter, one piece of bread. When Leon came to the US, he got a job as a mechanic and every night after work, he bought a sandwich, went to a movie, and taught himself how to speak English.

Well, we bought out Leon. He was about $30,000 out of trust, which means cars were sold and the bank had not been paid for them.

Leon thought he was slick. He was working with a piece of shit banker, Pete Gerald, at the Hudson United Bank. They figured they could knock us out quickly, so they pulled a surprise car check and we were fucked. We scrambled, raised the money in one night, and paid the bank which foiled Leon and Pete's plans of taking us out. Then we were forced to make friends with the enemy, Pete Gerald.

The Camelot conspiracy having failed, Leon decided to go to Israel to set up his retirement, which was his ultimate plan.

He always had stomach pain, which we thought was from all the coffee and cigarettes. Then he got sick in Israel. They cut him open, sewed him shut and told him to go back to the US to settle his affairs. I went to see Leon in the hospital and he said to me, "Lou, a man can only wear one suit at a time." I always remember those words, but never lived by them.

While we were partners, we were moving so many cars British Leland offered us their full line of cars: Jaguar, Triumph, Austin and MG. We were required to give them a separate facility, so we rented a showroom across from where we were operating. Business got very slow and we started to slip, so we sold the Fiat store. The Fiat franchise was hot and we had an option to buy the building, which made it more attractive to buyers.

At Camelot, things cooled, business sucked, we went deeper in debt, and we got caught in another car check. That fucking weasel Pete Gerald folded like a cheap card table. All that money we paid him to protect us went down the drain. A meeting was called with British Leyland and The Hudson United Bank, where Pete Gerald offered a loan to bail us out.

He basically said, "If you look the wrong way, you're done." He was right; he had us by the balls. The whole thing didn't seem right. So I pulled the plug just in time. I asked Bernie to step outside the meeting and told him the partnership wasn't working and I wanted to dissolve it. He said he had the controlling shares and would buy me out.

Well, I walked away. Bernie never bought me out or fixed the problems. I was charged with numerous counts, including delivering cars without titles. I needed a job, so I went to work for Manny for a short time, but I was harassed by Camelot creditors on a daily basis.

In fact, I recall when I got the call from Pete at the bank that the total owed was $53,000. I sang to the tune of the Burger King commercial (hold the pickles, hold the lettuce, special orders don't upset us), "Hold the titles, grab the keys, we're out of trust 50Gs." Pretty ballsy for a broke bust-out, facing serious charges and jail.

Bernard R Treich (aka Bernie, Bumpy, Boom Boom)

While I have numerous "My Most Unforgettable Character Stories," Bernie ranks in the top ten. Bernie would "wake and bake" (smoke a joint as he opened his eyes). He was one of those individuals who could conduct his business better stoned than most people sober. In addition to pot, he liked booze, but his Achilles heel and ultimate demise was Coke.

Camelot Motors was across the street from McLoins Midway Tavern. Everybody at McLoins had their own stools. Me and Bernie being the new guys had standing room at the cash register. As you walked the length of the bar, staring you in the face was a poster of the bars patron saint Archie Bunker, getting my drift?

So it's Saturday morning, March 17, Bernie says "let's get a drink." I said, "Bumpy, its 9 Am." his reply was "it's Saint Patty's day, come on." We had taken the precaution to cover our two floor to ceiling plate glass windows, which had an Italian flag on one and the Union Jack with giant shamrocks on the other, so as the drunks left the bar they didn't take out their prejudice and anger.

Our drink of the day choice was shots of Jamison's with Irish coffee chasers. All the places were set for lunch and the party favors included plastic green derbies and clay pipes.

The regulars were always taunting "You have any of that funny tobacco, BOOM BOOM"? By 2pm everybody in the bar was annihilated so Bernie loaded all the pipes with pot. Archie's disciples all got high. I was told by the bartenders Sunday morning after Mass they all acted like this never happened

Supplemental Income

While I had Camelot, things were real good. I spent most nights in Manhattan at the best clubs and restaurants: Hippopotamus, Directua, Sign of The Dove, Grotta Azzurra, Vincent's Clam Bar, Umberto's Clam House, Bill Chan's Gold Coin, Maxwell's Plum, Ali Baba, PJ Clarks, Elaine's, Chateau Henry the Eighth (home to the Metropolitan Opera stars) and the best and hottest after hours clubs. I was hanging out with celebrities, Wise Guys, etc. My supply of primo coke added to my popularity.

When things started to turn, I revved up the Supplemental Income.

Guns were always a demand item, as was porn. Remember, this was before the days of Beta and VCRs. Porn carried serious penalties, if caught, but the spread was huge, and a 50 foot reel of 8 millimeter film was small. You could put 10 in a paper bag that looked like a lunch and collect $500 to $750.

In the early 1970s, I had a lucrative pot business. Then, when I was introduced to cocaine, it was like the films: small packages that turned big profits. I had a Columbian connection who would call once a month, and it was bonus time. I operated independently, with the aura of having backing. It's all about posture.

I always had a good paying legit job; these other ventures were supplementary income. When business was bad, or I was in a crack, I went to what I knew. Over the years I experienced more downs than ups, so I did whatever I had to. I discovered Life is like a round of Golf or a game of Pool, the strategy is as you make a shot try to set up your next shot, so on all my deals I tried to position myself for future opportunities.

Always Grant an Accomodation

For example, I knew this chick from a bar that I hung out. She was a regular, but like with most people, I kept my distance. "Hello, goodbye, how are you?" was enough. She approached me once, saying someone told her I might be able to help her. She heard that I could get things done.

"Like what?" I asked.

She explained that her ex-boyfriend had taken some compromising pictures of her and now he wanted her to pay to get them back. So I told her I'd look into it. A few days later, I walked into the bar and handed her an envelope with the photos. She said she was embarrassed that I had seen the pictures, but I told her I didn't look at them, they were none of my concern. When I left her ex-boyfriend, he assured me that there were no copies and emphatically said he never wanted to see her or me again.

"Thank you, thank you, and thank you. I don't know how I'm going to pay you back," she said.

"Forget about it, I'm glad I could help," was my reply.

That gesture solidified my image. Everybody in the bar heard the story and tried to get close to me, but I kept them at arm's length. Which added to the mystique.

Over the years, I made friends and acquaintances with guys from various factions and levels. I always granted an accommodation and never asked for anything, and that was huge.

"Lou is a good guy and never has his hand out." See, contrary to popular belief, Wise Guys don't like to pay.

Houston: Boom or Bust

After the Camelot debacle and the harassment at Rallye Motors, I decided it would be best if I got out of Dodge. Against my better judgement, I didn't want to be beholden, but Sandi really wanted to stay in New Jersey. So I went to Uncle Ernie for help.

After our meeting, he never returned my calls. Just as well 'cause four years later he went to jail. Guess who would have been with him?

I had been to Houston, Texas for the 1972 Super Bowl and for a friend's wedding. I knew the city was vibrant and growing, and I could get a fresh start.

I called an old friend I met in New Jersey, Frank Emmette. Frank was raised in Dickenson, Texas, and lived in Houston. He got me a job at Gillman Pontiac/GMC/Honda in Houston. Immediately, I started to make money and put my former life behind me.

I was well respected by the Gillman management and my colleagues. I received a call from Hingham's Cadillac, offering me a job selling Cadillac/Rolls Royce. What a break. When I resigned from Gillman, I was told by some of the old timers I was the only salesman that they ever saw approached by the

A WISER GUY

Gillman management to stay. I was flattered and explained I knew I was being considered for management, but frankly the team that was in place had about 10 years before retirement. So I went to Hingham's and started off great. Then the second gas crisis hit and back to odd and even days rationing. Nobody was buying Cadillac/Rolls Royce.

I was screwed.

A guy I worked with, Billy, told me he had a home for coke, so I reached out and took a chance. This deal would give me breathing room. I had the money up front and the buyers were anxious. Billy was on his way to deliver when the phone rang. It was Billy, scared to death. The product was laced with speed. They were holding him hostage till I came with the money. No time to get a gun. I knew where he lived, so I went to Larry, the supplier's house. That's not the way it works, but he wasn't playing by the rules.

As Larry opened the door, I screamed at him, and to my surprise, here comes a nasty German Shepard. He contained the dog, asked me in, and asked for an explanation.

I told him, "There's no discussion. I want the money, and when I straighten out the mess, you will get your speed back."

Not too many people knew the one thing that I was deathly afraid of was bad dogs. That night, the dog and Larry would have died if I hadn't gotten the money. I took the money, bailed out Billy, and left the speed on Larry's doorstep.

Associated Industries

Now I'm totally screwed.

Nobody is selling cars to speak of, so I started wholesaling. That wasn't working 'cause all the dealers were slow. I called an old friend, Gary Hays, who was a crew chief at Sam White Oldsmobile. Gary said to come over, pick out a demo, and go to work. It was around Thanksgiving, and I needed to try to make a Christmas for my daughter Jennifer.

I sold 3 cars in 3 days. Then I got the phone call from Joe Poindexter, Frank Emmette's father-in-law and the man who became my friend, mentor, fan and partner. He asked me what time I got off and told me to stop by the house.

Joe had a fabrication shop that made recording cabs for seismic exploration and had merged his company with a group called Associated Industries. He told me he needed a salesman, and I was him. I told Joe I was flattered, but knew nothing about his business. He said all he wanted me to do was entertain his customers, eat, drink and party, ultimately getting the opportunity to bid their work.

Could this be happening? A real job with a paycheck and an expense account in a world that is reserved mainly for scientists. What did I do to deserve this?

A WISER GUY

Joe gave me a call list and told me I needed to turn 10 people on the list into Associated Industries customers. So I went about the task. What Joe neglected to tell me was one of the seven key partners in Associated had pissed off the principles of all 10 companies. Well, I turned 6 of the 10 in six months, and when any of the other salesmen were making lunch dates, the customers asked if Lou was coming.

The word spread quickly that Lou spared no expense. When you were with me it wasn't beer and burgers; it was steak, fine whiskey and wines. My first month with Joe, I turned in a $2500 expense account.

Isabel, the bookkeeper, asked, "Mr. Poindexter, Lou is new and you put him on the road?" Joe P replied, "No, Isabell, that's all in town. I'm afraid to put the boy on the road." But I quickly gained recognition.

Even Joe Rogers, who was chairman of Associated, told me he had told Joe P to get rid of me. After all, I was a car peddler. But Joe R became one of my biggest supporters.

Six months after my hire, Joe P called me in and said, "You're getting quite a name out there. In the next few months people are going to come with offers. I ask for right of first refusal."

So I replied, "I've been approached already, so why don't we structure a deal we are both happy with and I won't even listen to any offers. I can just say, 'thank you but I'm happy with Joe P and Associated'."

We restructured my deal, which included a paycheck, commissions, a Cadillac Seville and an expense account that I could use for personal reasons.

Who was better than me?

I did great. I even was a card- carrying member of The Society of Exploration Geophysicists. I had finally become the man I strove to be: liked, respected and sought after. I was helping in design and innovative changes during the late 1970s oil boom. I lived up to Joe P's belief in me and made the industry take notice.

One day, while flying to Denver with Joe R, he told me Associated had just signed a letter of intent with a shell company from NY and (which I knew because I put together the celebration party for 25-30 people at the Houston Palm, you should have seen that month's expense account) if I stayed with the company, I would get the presidency in 2 to 3 years.

But Joe R and Joe P thought I had more to offer and said they would like to back me if I decided to go out on my own.

Selex

I told him about my idea for a luxury car rental business with Caddies and Mercedes. People of means felt more comfortable in an automobile they were familiar with.

In the 1970s, car controls were all over the place (wipers, lights, radio) so if you were in a strange town, in a strange car, trying to find your way around in a rental car was difficult if not impossible.

I had recently been in LA and had a meeting at a posh restaurant. As I pulled up in a Ford Fairmont, all I could see were Mercedes, Porches, Rolls, etc. Split second decision: park around back or valet. What the fuck, everybody knows I'm from Houston. Of course I took care of all the valets, which was not commensurate with my rental car, but I came out with a 2 million dollar order. My ego would have been nurtured if I was in a Caddy.

Joe R flipped over my luxury car idea and gave my pro forma to Ted Batek, their partner and accountant. Joe P, Joe R and Ted backed my Selex Motor Car Systems. I could not believe I finally had the opportunity to really show my real talent and worth.

Selex was set up with limited market expansion or possible franchise in mind. The startup was pricy because we were preparing our business for the future. We bought a building 7 minutes from Houston Intercontinental Airport (George Bush Intercontinental Airport), poured an acre of concrete, decorated to the hilt, and installed an extra wide canopy that covered two cars to ensure our customers were never exposed to the elements.

The computer program we had specially designed for Selex cost $30,000. Today you could get a comparable program anywhere, for corks. We advertised in US Air, Pan Am and Continental in-flight magazines. They were the major carriers to Houston; the cost was a "mere" $7,000 per month.

Things started off great. In addition to the business from Intercontinental Airport, we had a long list of private jet customers who we picked up on the tarmac. We had a direct dial courtesy phone in baggage claim. Customers were instructed to walk out of baggage claim and our Caddy limo shuttle car would be waiting. We bought a car phone ($5,000 and $1.00 per minute.) The driver opened the door and loaded the luggage. When he pulled under the canopy, he asked the customer to step inside to complete the paper work, and then transferred their luggage. The service went beyond first class.

We bought our cars locally from friends in the business. I received a call from Cadillac, they wanted to visit. When they came in they were perplexed because National Car Rental was renting Caddies. But their cars were plain vanilla. Our cars had vinyl tops, full power, split leather seats, tape players, wire wheels, etc.

They asked why. I told them I was not in the car rental business; I was in the used car manufacturing business. The hottest cars on the used car market at that time were 1 year old Caddies and Mercedes.

I bought Caddies for $200 over pure invoice, curtailed them (paid down} at $200 per month, with the rental income. We now owned the Caddies for $2200 under invoice, and we sold them for $2200 to $2500 profit. We could not get as good a deal on Mercedes, but the profit worked similarly.

We were moving along, exploring franchising and or expansion, and then the bottom fell out. The price of oil plummeted. Interest was 18%. The peso was worthless, so there went our affluent Mexican trade. Business started to dry up. Our lucrative leasing business collapsed. People stopped coming to Houston. There was limited business travel. And to compound the problem, Ted had cross-pledged our assets with their other businesses they had interest in.

Once again, a banker pulled the plug. It was Lovett Baker, brother of James Baker, former Secretary of State.

My dream floated away

I hate fucking bankers

I lost Selex, but Joe P, Joe R and Ted Batek lost everything. Joe P always said, he got his 100 K upfront, like the other partners in Associated, and he never got one cent of earn out, but he was "Queen for a Day."

I had to liquidate and during that time, I was hired by Associated Industries. The new management thought they could turn it around. Ha! But I was drawing a pay.

New Jersey Bound

In 1983, I put my Houston house up for sale. I got lucky because the buyer was from Kansas City and I had the only house in the area with aluminum siding, which he liked.

I walked away with $5,000, plus what I had stashed, and headed back home to New Jersey, where I worked at a couple of car lots to make a pay.

Willowbrook Nissan

I was recommended to the owner of a Nissan store and was hired as the Used Car Manager. I worked there about a month. Then I came in one morning and the GM asked me if I closed the night before. He knew I did, I was the manager on duty. He then asked about receipted money. I explained all the deals, including $2200 in cash. I had counted the cash, put it in a bank envelope, and watched the salesman deposit it in the drop safe and use the ram board to insure the drop.

That afternoon, I was summoned upstairs to be interviewed by two detectives. Good cop, bad cop. They are so lame and predictable.

So the good cop says, "Lou, what do you think happened?"

"I've already told you everything I know," I replied. He asked if I would be willing to take a lie detector.

"Absolutely," I said without hesitation. "When all the employees and vendors who conduct business here, including the owner, take a test, hook me up."

The cop smiled. He knew I wasn't an amateur.

He politely thanked me and I walked down the hall and down the stairs. During that short walk, I decided I had to leave. They were looking to pin somebody. Even though I was clean, I didn't need to be watching over my shoulder. So I walked up to the GM, handed in my keys and asked for a ride home. He questioned my decision; I explained I didn't like the climate.

About 2 years later, when I was at Garfield Chrysler, one of the Willow Brook employees stopped by to see me. He said he had to tell me they finally found out what happened to the money. The bookkeeper, 20 year employee, was caught with her hand in the cookie jar and confessed to all of her thefts.

Garfield

After the Nissan store, I went to a small Chrysler dealership in Garfield, NJ, Garfield Chrysler Plymouth. I was paid mostly cash, which was good because I had a bunch of bill collectors and the IRS breaking my balls.

Garfield was an experience. The owner was a brilliant engineer who bought the dealership for his own ego, but also to avenge the fucking his father got in 1939. See, his dad was the service manager, the main source of revenue, and built the building that housed the dealership. As happens too many times in life, the guys at the top believe they made the success and find guys like the service manager dispensable, especially when they have to ante up on their promises, in this case a partnership.

I helped in all aspects of the operation, but brought the most value keeping creditors away and running a $180,000 float, recalling my Camelot days.

During my tenure at GCP, I met some real characters. Steve was a local bookmaker under the Lucchese banner. I would let him come in and use the dealership phone to conduct business. Tony, the owner, would always ask why Steve was using the phone, and I would say he was shopping a car I was trying to trade. When I made a deal, I would tell Tony that Steve helped us.

Steve was a trip. He was well connected to local politicians. He took action. He hustled cars and had the best clocker in the business on his payroll. He would have 5 or 6 good years and then he would take a pinch. His last pinch, he was doing business in a coffee shop, and when he came out he was jumped by a UPS guy, a mailman, and a laborer (all undercover OCB officers.) Steve had all his utility meters on the outside of his house and no one other than his family was allowed in his house unless he was home.

Then there was Petey, who started out with Pete LaPlaca and was loaned to the Colombo's and there he stayed. Petty who was as bad as they come. But he was more observant and savvy than most.

Once he was invited to a yacht for a party. His Capo and crew thought they had a mullet with this yacht owner. But when Petey arrived, he noticed the owner wearing cheap Thom McCann's and sporting a Timex. Petey excused himself and left.

Later, his Capo,"Beansy," and several of the crew were indicted. Petey was indicted because "Beansy" was recorded implicating him. During the trial, Beansey had a heart attack and died. The judge said to Petey, it was with great remorse he had to let a parasite like him off because he could not face his accuser. Believe it or not, Petey told me he loved Beansy so much he would have gladly taken his chances, if only Beansy had lived.

One time, this kid came by, trying to collect for a landau top we had purchased. I told him, like the other collectors, they would be paid in 30 days, maybe sooner, but on my word in 30. This douche bag got in my face. I grabbed his arm across his body and slid him out the door.

So I got a call from his boss who questioned my actions. I explained, "Don't ever send a boy who doesn't have a clue on a collection."

Next thing I see, there's an Eldorado, with a gold package, grill, continental kit and Vogues. Out steps a sawed-off guinea runt with a bad perm and a Members Only jacket. He's going to smooth this over and attempt to collect.

I politely explained, "There's a right way and a wrong way to handle matters. The kid should never been sent, the boss is a jerk-off, and you can expect payment in about 27 days."

The perm tried to be friendly, dropping the hint that they hang out at Funzi's place. Frank (Funzi) Terri was acting boss of the Genovese family. Like I give a shit.

Hey, I could make a call if I had to. And besides, who was sitting behind me? Petey, who asked me if I needed an assist. Petey would have shot him on the grounds of stupidity.

Petey brought us a lot of business and a lineup of interesting characters, including one of his close allies, Philly Rags, a ranking Bonnano guy from East Harlem.

I will never forget the day at the dealership when Steve, Petey and some of his guys were in attendance with Bishop Rodhimer from the Paterson diocese, who we sold a car to. They all chatted and got along famously. I thought to myself I had all bases covered. Heaven and Earth

We had a good run in Garfield. I ran a ring of shoplifters who used stolen credit cards to acquire merchandise that had been ordered. I got 50 cents on the dollar, they got 25 cents on the dollar, and the purchaser got a great deal. I always advised the buyer not to try repairs under warranty.

Don't Trust Nobody — But You Can Trust Lou

One time, Mr. A, the owner of the Chrysler store, reneged on a deal with Petey. Not a good idea. A guy who knew Petey well once said to me, "If you get the wrong guy mad at you, you need to get out of town. If you get Petey mad at you, you need to get off the planet."

Petey came looking for Mr. A, who was not there, and Petey was so pissed, he fired a couple of shots into a radiator to make his point. Mr. A ran to the cops.

I called Petey to tip him off and he told me to meet him at one of his haunts. As soon as I walked in, two guys scurried from the bar. They were detectives, and I'm sure they didn't want me to ID them. The stupid part was they couldn't arrest him on hearsay, and if they did, Mr. A would have had a real problem.

Remember, "Don't trust nobody."

Petey had told Philly Rags of my pedigree and that I could be trusted. I accommodated Philly on numerous occasions, as I did for Petey, increasing my stock and opening avenues that may have otherwise been closed.

It is always good to be able to drop a name with confidence, knowing all it could get you was a thumbs up, but that translated to, "You're OK and can be trusted."

Yeah I know, "don't trust nobody." If more of these guys subscribed there would be fewer guys in witness protection and jail.

Soon after the incident with Mr. A and the cops, Petey's boyhood friend Ronnie, who was living in Florida, and who Petey always looked out for, got into a jackpot(jam) and tried to set up Petey to save his own skin. Once again, Petey was too smart for them and spotted the cops immediately, foiling the attempt.

Florida Trash & The Horseshit King

It was time for my own fresh start, so I moved to Florida and rented an apartment in Deerfield Beach. I was working for a Jewish funeral home, selling pre-need funerals, when Uncle Ange called. He had been talking to Carmine Franco (Uncle Sonny, Papa Smurf) who said Mario Goffredo was setting up a roll-off company in Deerfield Beach and needed help.

I knew who Mario was. He had been the head of the Trade Waste Association in NJ and when the business took a blow from the law, the decision was to remove Mario and replace him with the lily white former mayor of Maywood, NJ, to try to give an air of respectably.

Mario was given a defunct route in Maryland. He did what he did best, turned it into a moneymaker and sold out for $3 million. Of course, the greedy fucks in NJ were looking for a cut. He had been given nothing, but now they wanted a share.

Louis (Streaky) Gatto was in charge in NJ. Streaky finally got upped, after many years of faithful service. Mario fought hard, but eventually had to kick up some, though not as much as they wanted.

Mario had friends in several families. John Digilio once asked him how many flags he was flying. Mario always relished in the fact he was close to guys from all the families and South Florida is Wise Guy Heaven. I always wondered why Uncle Ernie came to Florida after he was paroled, and could get violated if he was in the same building with other Wise Guys. There's as many, if not more, Wise Guys and associates in Florida than the whole New York metropolitan area. In fact, a friend of Uncle Ernie's told me several times they were in restaurants when Ernie saw someone on the list walk in and he immediately got up and left.

Mario and me hit it off great. He was off the wall, but crazy like a fox. His brother-in-law was Rocco Miraglia, Joe Colombo's right hand guy. Mario was on his way to get his Block Captain badge for the Italian American Civil Rights League, when Joe Colombo got shot. Mario thought it was a primer to a button. He ran with old and young Wise Guys and wannabes and was enamored by The Life. Everybody we met, Mario would tell them about Uncle Ernie, which bumped my stature in those circles.

Mario told me he needed to build his roll off business. He gave me some cards and said, "You know what to do." I started placing cans, and then Hurricane Andrew hit. We were sent trucks and drivers from Maryland and NJ, and a slew of cans. Mario said he needed me full time. We were extremely busy and ran dump trailers, walking floors, and push-outs, all night, 7 nights a week, from Miami to Pompano for FEMA. The abuses and disarray of the Andrew clean up made the government smart; there will never be a score like that again.

Mario's Uncle Dominick owned a huge garbage business in NY and NJ. He told Mario about an old neighbor, Vinny, who was running dump trucks, and he should look him up. Vinny was a bookmaker and close associate of Carlo Gambino. He was part of a virtually unknown squad of trusted non-made members who reported directly to Carlo, who wanted to ensure he had their loyalty and they couldn't be tainted by disgruntled underlings.

Vinny, upon getting out of jail, was informed by his attorney about RICO. Carlo was dead, so that's when Vinny decided to look for a lower key business, like trucking. He moved to Florida and made friends with workers at Pompano Park Race Track, and got close to the superintendent of plant and grounds. He found this guy's weakness, got him on the pad, and finagled the rights to haul and dispose of all the horse manure. After meeting him, I crowned him the "Horseshit King," a name he wasn't fond of, but all the guys got a kick out of it.

We were operating in a yard that had 4 offices, 2 baths, and garage for 3 trucks, along with parking for several others. During the Andrew cleanup, we helped NJ and NY guys that needed phones, secretarial, a garage to work in, etc. Vinny brought around a lot of retired and active Gambino guys. We were asked to babysit the son of a Connected Guy who was getting into trouble in New York. His father bought him a dump truck and we helped him get work.

Mafia Wife

One day Mario yelled, "Hey Louie, come in here." Our offices were side by side, and I knew he had someone in with him, because I heard talking. I walked in, leaned with my back to the wall, and Mario said, "Louie, say hello to Linda."

So I said, "Hi Linda."

She replied, "Hi Louie, I'm a widow."

Flabbergasted, I said, "I'm sorry, Linda."

And she continued, "Sammy Gravano killed my husband.

Wow, not to use the cliché, but "every time I think I'm out, they pull me back in."

I later told Mario I didn't like this, she may be working for the feds. We weren't doing anything wrong, but the feds are known for setting you up.

Linda was selling these special made colorful business cards that went into racks in delicatessens, dry cleaners, etc. The price was $750 and Mario asked my opinion. He could care less, he wanted to date her. He wanted my endorsement so he had an excuse to buy the cards.

They started dating and he brought her around the wrong places. We got a visit, and he was told to do whatever he wanted to, but don't bring her around.

The chick was Linda Milito, wife of Louie Milito (and author of Mafia Wife and Mafia Widow.)

Several years later, I was having dinner with Sandi when Linda walked in, ran up to me, and gave me a hug. I introduced her and when she left, I explained. No explanation necessary, my wife already knew the story.

Perception

When I was with Mario, he was always concerned about people's perceptions. One night, we were at Villa Peron in Hollywood, Florida. We were with our wives and were meeting the daughter, and her husband, of the owner of a major trash management company. They gave us a lot of good paying work. Emphasis on good paying. Most management companies squeeze you 'till you're losing. And most small garbage companies aren't smart enough to figure it out until it's too late and the piranhas win.

Villa Peron was owned by one of three brothers, the other brothers owned Pier 5 in Hollywood and Trulo's in Pompano — all Wise Guy meeting places where Mario would throw dinner parties for visiting dignitaries. These restaurants were loaded with wannabes hoping to get noticed or get a chance to kowtow to a recognized mobster, who by the way wouldn't give them the time of day.

We were at the bar waiting for our guests and this sawed off runt keeps bumping me. I asked him politely not to do it and finally I told him the next time would be his last. I had become used to this type of behavior — assholes always looking to take a chance with me.

A WISER GUY

In my 20s and 30s, I would fight with little provocation. But after my run in with a knife, I mellowed slightly, and used more discretion.

Before I could say another word, Mario jumped between us to calm things. He pissed me off. Mario admitted he had no idea who the guy was, but he had a feeling.

I said, "Feeling my ass." The guy was an asshole, no matter who he was.

One time, we had a deadbeat roofer who was dodging us, so Mario, me and Vinny went to collect. When we got there, the door was open, so I walked in. Nobody in sight. I walked through and still nobody. I made my way back to the office, where I commandeered cell phone lists and titles for all the employees.

As I walked out, I was surrounded by 6 guys. I held my own, especially knowing Mario and Vinny had me covered. Vinny was now out of the car, yelling, "Louie come on let's go."

"I'll be right there," I said.

Vinny yelled back, emphatically, "Now Louie."

I had determined, by talking to the party of six, who was the guy with the money and when and where I could find him.

When I got to the car, Vinny explained the reason he was so adamant was I was trespassing, and they could shoot me with probably no repercussions. Outside the building, no rules applied. I believe the guys saw the sinister-looking black Mercedes with limo tint and kind of hid till they saw me, and surrounded me, until they heard Vinny and saw Mario, realizing I was not alone. The following morning, we were paid in full.

One night, after one of Mario's dinner parties, me and Vinny were at the bar when a guy invites Vinny to his table. According to Vinny, he had to go; the guy was a Ranking Member.

Vinny and another guy had a beef and Vinny settled it his way, embarrassing him in front of a bunch of guys. This Ranking Guy was going to take up the matter. I refused to leave. Vinny assured me he was OK and had to do this by himself. The next day, he told me how much he appreciated me wanting to stay, but I had to learn to listen.

Franchising

Mario owned a trash management company in NJ that handled the waste for the Federated Department Stores nationally. After the Andrew cleanup, thanks to Mario, we were doing a lot of compactor work, which pissed off the established haulers. Florida has franchises that usually allow only one hauler to work a town. I met a local government guy who turned me onto a Florida recycling statute and we started fighting franchises. We made enough noise, a local company bought out Mario, and we went to Philly.

Later in my career in Florida, when I spoke to any group, I always incorporated the following: "It strikes me funny that you only allow one hauler per town. Down here it's called franchising. Where I come from, it's called racketeering."

Philly

In Philly, I went to work for Carmine Franco at AAA Waste and Recycling. Mario started a roll-off company and commenced to make friends.

Philly was an interesting place. As they say, nice place to visit, but I didn't want to live there. A lot of politics at AAA Recycling and when I don't want to play, it's time to go.

During my time at Triple A, we were being monitored by the feds (snapping pictures, helicopters overhead, etc.), which wasn't the first time I had been photographed, and it added to the posture.

What I found most interesting about Philly was the number of people who would tell others they were told to use us, and that came from Carmine's reputation as an associate and major earner.

Carmine pissed off a lot of people, including a former partner, Sal Avena, who was an attorney. Sal's father, John (Big Nose) Avena, was the Philly boss who was clipped years before. Sal knew how it works, but the dumbass sued Carmine.

An FBI bug recorded a conversation between Sal Avena and Sal Profaci: "Carmine is a major earner, besides Goodfellas don't sue Goodfellas. Goodfellas kill Goodfellas."

Mario made an alliance with future Philly boss Joe (Uncle Joe) Ligambi, which garnered the Philly produce market for Mario. He put Uncle Joe on the pay roll for $1000 a week and health insurance for his family. Mario told his son Greg, "Take care of your mother and sister and honor Uncle Joe's contract," which brought Greg grief, scrutiny and court appearances.

Mario was always ready to pick up a tab, but years later he loved to come back to Florida and have me meet him and his associates, and impress them when I got the tab. See, I was on an expense account, and Mario played it to the hilt.

Realization

I was 44 in Philly, working for Carmine and out collecting. I walked into a workingman's bar in a rough neighborhood and was the only white guy in the bar. I got some evil stares, especially in light of being dressed in my normal attire, suit and overcoat.

I asked the bartender for the owner, who invited me into his office. I got paid in full and had every eye in the joint fixed on me till I got out the door.

That was the day I had an epiphany. The respect and/or fear that we once enjoyed was not guaranteed, and while I had been in numerous similar situations and collected thousands for a lot of people, I finally realized putting myself in danger wasn't worth it.

Don't Fuck with Lou

So it was 1993, I was back in Florida and minding my own business, looking for something to do, when I was contacted by two guys I met during the Andrew cleanup. They were setting up a recycling yard and roll-off business in Pompano and asked for my help. One of the partners, Phil, was a world class scumbag. He fucked everybody he came in contact with, but he paid me cash and the skim was great.

One afternoon, a car came flying through the gate into the yard, and 4 guys hopped out, forming a semicircle around Phil. I came down the stairs and walked up to them.

Lou: What's the problem?

Guys: This no good motherfucker is trying to take our work. He's a scumbag piece of shit.

Lou: Calm down, I'm sure we can work this out.

So one guy leans in and whispers into the leader's ear.

Leader: Fuck this, let's go.

The guys got back into their car and screeched down the street.

Phil: Thanks man, I really appreciate you standing up for me.

Lou: Forget about it, let's lock up.

Well, those 4 guys became my friends and I did some work for them.

The guy who did the whispering became very close to me. Years later he told me, "I told my uncle, I don't know who this guy is, but I don't like it." Once again, posture. Over the years we all agreed I should have let them take care of business with Phil. Oh well.

The Art of Collection

The general population has always been beguiled with fame, celebrity and mobsters. When I was collecting, I would hear from several people about a friend of theirs that could be mutual. My standard reply to this, and the suggestion of a cup of coffee or lunch, was handled with a, "Thank you, but I did not come here for coffee, chit chat, or to discuss friends. I'm here to resolve the matter." I was courteous, but to the point. Whenever someone dropped a name, I would tell them, "Go see whoever you gotta go see." (After you pay me.)

Amazingly, I always left with the money or a reasonable payment plan, which was always complied with. I batted 1,000 and never used a bat or other means of persuasion.

One time, I had an elderly guy who was slightly demented threaten me, and he dropped a name. I handled him a little differently. I left, and circumvented the people he was talking about and I contacted his cousin, who was aligned with that faction. I told him I didn't care either way, but for his sake he should know. The cousin asked the amount the old guy owed and paid me, which I did not expect, and thanked me for handling the incident the way I did. He assured me I would not have to deal with the old guy again.

I was always on the front line when it came to collecting money. This one time, I've got this contractor who's not paying, so I call him on the phone.

"Hey, Joe, it's Lou. You promised me money Friday, today's Monday, what the fuck?"

"I'm sorry Lou," Joe said, "but I got this guy that does my block paneling and the prick won't finish this big job in Boca. The homeowner's breaking my balls. I can't get paid till I finish the job. You need to get paid and I can't get this bastard to even call me."

So I got the guy's name and location and drove out to the building where he had a bay for his custom woodworking business. I banged on the door, banged on the garage door, and someone from the next door office came out. I asked where his neighbor was, and he said the guy's never around. So I got a piece of paper from my car, wrote my name and number on it, and gave it to the neighbor. "When you see him, he needs to call me. I'm a friend of Joe's.

I went back to the office and a couple of hours later, Joe shows up with a bottle of Royal Salute and asks, "What did you do?

"Whata you talking about?" I replied.

"This asshole finds me on a job, fumbling all around, apologizing and promised to be in Boca first thing in the morning, and the job finished by Friday. And I will be able to tighten you up on Monday. Thank you, Mr. Lou."

"Joe, I swear all I did was left a message."

"Yeah, I'm sure you did. Thanks, I'll see you Monday," Joe said.

I really did nothing, but the story spread and the message was, "Don't fuck with me or people I do business with." Once again raising my stock.

As I say, it's all about posture. A timely favor or dropped name really helps.

Louis's Temperament Barometer

To this day, every time I have a bad work day or financial problem, I chant, "I should have been a pharmacist. Mama told me, 'Lou Lou, be a pharmacist'."

Anyone who knows me knows the number one way to ascertain my bad mood is when I chant, "I should have been a pharmacist."

If I am in a seriously bad mood, or having an exceptionally bad time or day, the chant becomes, "I shoulda been a fuckin' pharmacist!"

And if you ever hear, 'I SHOULDA BEEN A MOTHERFUCKIN' PHARMACIST!' get out of my way.

When I drift into thought, usually over my morning coffee, I think of my life choices. My voice led to several suggestions that I go into broadcasting. With my argumentative nature, tenacity, my conviction to prove my point, and grasp of the English language, I was told I should be a lawyer.

And of course, Mama is always there with the words that have been with me 59 years, "Lou Lou, you should be a pharmacist,"

When I come back to where I am in life at the moment, and reflect on some bad breaks, some self-inflicted problems, and fate, I rationalize.

I never acquired the gambling vice. Probably due to the economic devastation and heartache I have witnessed it causes, coupled with I hate losing and work too hard for my money. But I have gambled with the biggest chip ever: my life. My job choices, business choices. Always wanting to parlay my current status and reach for the elusive shining star or brass ring.

While I have had a bumpy ride, I don't know if I would have been happy in any one occupation. I have an extremely short attention span. If I have an interest in something, I can't get enough knowledge. If I have no interest, I can't be force' fed. In either case, I move on rapidly.

The question remains, could I have picked a career that I would have stayed with, and after forty years retire? Could I go the pharmacy every day and count pills, mix potions, lotions, salves, creams, and smile at all who entered? Could I deal with vendors and ride out the corporate takeover of the hometown pharmacy? Or would I have folded to the pressure? Would I have been another Walgreen, Rexall, or Eckerd and built an empire? Could I have handled the challenges and rise above whatever came my way? I have survived more than my fair share of crash and burns, but if I had become a pharmacist would I have been in a position to do the things that got me through my downs and every crisis in the life I've lived?

In any case, I will never know. My gut tells me that my destiny card was dealt and I was born to play this hand. An interesting phenomenon in my business life is when I'm out of chips I win a small pot, but just large enough to ante up one more time.

Mr DiVita

I tried several times to get away from the things I was involved in and get a job that paid enough that I could turn down any tempting supplemental income. I took my training and went to work for a Whitebread recycling company.

That job gave me a professional image and put me into local, county and state politics. I was a featured speaker and actually became a recognized contributor to the industry and government.

Finally, I had gained real respect, except from the average asshole. I was once introduced by a then member of the Florida House as, "Mister DiVita. He's Italian, he's from New Jersey, and he's in the trash business. Need I say more?"

I laughed. What else could I do?

Turning 50

When I turned 50, I said I didn't want to ever go to jail, but if I had to it wouldn't be that bad. I wouldn't have to fight for my life 'cause no one wants to fuck a fifty year old in the ass.

Seriously, at 50 ,I finally realized with the sophistication of the law, nothing is worth the chance. I will continue to do my best to stay in the fresh air.

A Different Road

Over the years, I made several attempts to succeed in the business world and for several reasons — many my own mistakes that I like to call the learning curve — my successes were short- lived. Like I say, you can't hit me with a left hook 'cause I've been hit by so many left hooks and hated it so much, I learned how to slip them. And of course, sometimes there were circumstances beyond my control.

When I got married and then when my daughter was born, I was doing pretty good. From 1969 until 1975, I thought I could rise above any obstacle, one way or another. I was particularly aware of and took precautions with everything I did, because now I had a wife and a daughter.

See, a huge part of my upbringing was I should earn and provide for my family, who I wanted to reap the spoils of my work. I was seldom home; I left early in the morning and came home late at night. The car business in those days required you work bell to bell to make sure everything was under control and to protect your territory. When I became a partner in Camelot, it became more important to be there during open hours and after hours and Sundays. When we had Camelot and the money was flowing in legitimately, the supplemental income was the icing on the cake. Money was going to my house, and even though we were operating on the float, and while we always had issues, I felt secure. And then I took my first tumble.

When I was little, I watched a lot of TV and was always fascinated by the TV preachers and faith healers. I believe you can learn from all sources and people. One motto that I subscribe to came from a TV preacher named Reverend Ike. He told his followers that God wanted him to have money, so his viewers should send him money so he could dress like he did and drive a" Cadillac car". Then he said, "Man says money is the root of all evil. Not so. The lack of money is the root of all evil." Truer words were never spoken. When people are hungry, they turn to crime.

Whoopi Goldberg said it in her act in the 1980s. During the Reagan presidency, while Nancy Reagan had her "Just Say No" campaign, Whoopi said, "Tell a kid living in a rat-infested ghetto apartment, who can make $10,000 a week selling drugs, to Just Say No."

There will always be criminals and crime and there will always be men who believe they can outsmart the system. But given the opportunity for a job and or a career that allows a man to provide for his family and gives him financial security, he will be complacent and follow the straight and narrow instead of the winding and never secure alternative path.

I went to Catholic school for seven of my first eight years of grammar school. The one year I missed was the fifth grade, when we had just moved to Fair Lawn and St. Ann's did not have space for me, so I spent a year in public school. I was a devout Catholic and, while I do not practice today, my beliefs and faith run deep. I don't subscribe to the belief that church attendance

A WISER GUY

fosters your faith. There is not a day in my life, consciously or subconsciously, that I don't call upon my teachings, coupled with my mother's words, "Follow the Golden Rule: do unto others as you would have them do unto you."

I live my life, for the most part, trying to do good, with the exception of when I'm faced with people or organizations that try my patience or attempt to hurt me in any way, especially financially. In keeping with that thought, I also, on a daily basis, consciously or subconsciously, call upon my dark side education and the glorification of what The Life used to be.

Yes, if things were different, if there was no RICO or the sophistication of law enforcement, if I could, I would go back to the dress, the glamor, the respect of the bygone days. Even though I was a little kid and a teen before it all went into the gutter, if I could go back, I would be 100% in The Life. But that was then, this is now.

I had a decent run, made a little money, garnered some respect in the business world, and today, when called upon, I consult in the waste and recycling business. I also own and operate a small fitness center that was supposed to be my retirement. I currently work seventy six hours a week. Work never bothered me, but some retirement!

Every day I take a few minutes and ponder what could have, or would have been, if I took a different road.

Growing up, I always wanted to be a Wise Guy, but I ended up "A Wiser Guy."

Nono

Nono's Recipes

Fresh summer tomato sauce!

Ingredients
1. 2-3 lbs. beefsteak tomatos
2. Extra virgin olive oil
3. 2-3 garlic cloves
4. Fresh basil
5. 1 lb. Fresh mozzarella
6. Parmesan cheese

Salt and pepper to taste

Chop tomatoes and place in large bowl with olive oil, chopped garlic and torn basil leaves season with salt and pepper. Cover with plastic and let flavors blend for a 2-3 hours at room temperature. Then add chopped mozzarella to bowl.

I use linguine for this recipe any pasta will do cook to al dente drain and immediately add to tomato mixture. Toss gently and use parmesan to taste as well as pepper. Place basil leaves on top. Delicious and simple

Macaroni Genovese (Veal Stew)

Ingredients
1. 2 lbs. veal stew meat
2. 2 onions grated
3. 1 lb. carrots grated
4. Fresh grated parmesan cheese
5. 1 lb. long thick pasta (Perciatelli)
Salt and Pepper to taste

Brown veal pieces in olive oil until well browned and place in bowl.

Lower heat and sauté the carrots and onions until soft 10-15 minutes.

Put veal and juices back in pan and add water just to cover and simmer on low heat about 1- 1&1/2 hours until tender.

Cook pasta until al dente, drain and place in pan with veal mixture, toss well and add extra virgin olive oil, parmesan pepper to taste.

Enjoy!

Gatto (Baked rice & beef dish)

This is a 2 step dish well worth the effort

Tomato sauce
1. 3-4 cans san marzano tomatoes placed in blended or crushed by hand
2. 1 large onion chopped
3. 4 garlic cloves minced
4. Italian seasonings
5. 3-4 lb. chuck roast

Sauté onions and garlic in a little olive oil until soft in a large saucepan or Dutch oven.

Add tomatoes and seasonings and start to simmer.

Cook sauce about an hour and put about 2-3 cups aside.

Season roast and add cook another 2-3 hours until meat is tender.

This step can be done a day ahead.

Rice
1. 3 cups cooked white rice (cooled)
2. 4 whole eggs
3. 6 tablespoons grated parmesan
4. Add plain sauce to rice mixture

After meat is tender take out and with two knives shred roast into thin pieces.

Grease a 9x13 casserole and sprinkle with Italian bread crumbs.

Place thick layer of rice mixture in dish and topped with thick layer of shredded meat and sauce, then another thick layer of rice. Lightly beat 2 egg whites and pour over top sprinkle with more bread crumbs.

Put a few pats of butter over and top and bake at 400 degrees for approximately 30-35 minutes until hot and bubbly.

Spinach Stuffing

Ingredients
1. 6 boxes frozen chopped spinach (10 oz.) thawed and completely drained
2. 4 large onions finely chopped
3. 8 large eggs lightly beaten
4. 2 or more cups fine bread crumbs
5. 4 cups grated parmesan cheese
6. Fresh chopped parsley

Salt and pepper to taste (remember cheese is salty)

In a large sauté pan sauté onions in extra virgin olive oil until soft on low heat about 10-15 minutes set aside and cool.

After spinach is drained place in large bowl and add eggs till lightly mixed.

Add about 2 cups cheese to cooled onion mixture.

Then add onions to spinach and eggs plus bread crumbs.

Finish off with more cheese to taste, parsley salt and pepper. Do not over mix.

I use this stuffing for Thanksgiving turkey and place directly in bird. Can also be used as a dressing baked in casserole dish.

Either way it is delicious!

Christmas Eve Fish Dinner

Ingredients
1. Striped Bass or Red Snapper
2. 4/6 Shrimp per person
3. 4/6 Clams per person
4. Clam Juice
5. Linguine
6. Olive Oil
4. Fresh Garlic
5. Fresh Parsley

Check with fish store on size of fish depending on how many people. Have fish scaled and guted, leave head on.

In a deep baking pan (enough to cover the fish with clam juice) put in about 1/2 cup olive oil.

Place fish in pan and coat it inside and out with chopped garlic (about 1/2 cup) and 1 cup chopped parsley.

Then pour in clam juice to cover fish.

Cover with foil and put on medium burners on stove top. Start your pasta water and drop in clams add linguine and about 2 minutes before you take out the linguine add shrimp and cover with foil. Once eyes of fish are pure white it is done.

Enjoy!!

Anne's Lemon Pie

Homemade Pie Crust
Ingredients
1. 1&1/4 cups flour
2. 1/4 teaspoon salt
3. 1/2 cups butter chilled and diced
4. 1/4 cups ice water

In large bowl combine flour and salt. Cut in butter until mixture resembles coarse crumbs. Stir in water 1 tablespoon at a time until mix forms ball.

Wrap in plastic and refrigerate 4 hours or overnight. Roll out dough and place in 9 inch pie pan.

Bake at 350 for 10-12 minutes weigh down with weights or beans and cool.

You can also use a refrigerated pie crust such as Pillsbury

Filling Ingredients
1. 11/2 cups sugar
2. 2 cups boiling water
3. 4 tablespoons cornstarch
4. 4 egg yolks (save whites for meringue)
5. 2 grated lemon rinds
6. 6 tablespoons lemon juice
7. 2 teaspoons butter

Mix cornstarch, flour and sugar add boiling water gradually stirring constantly. Cook 10 minutes at low heat. Add butter, egg yolks, rind and juice of lemon 2-3 minutes on low heat.

When filling is completely cool pour into baked shell.

Meringue

Bake eggs white until stiff and dry. Add 4-8 tablespoons sugar to whites depending on how sweet your taste is and spread on pie. Bake at 325 for 5-8 minutes.

www.ingramcontent.com/pod-product-compliance
Lightning Source LLC
Chambersburg PA
CBHW050529300426
44113CB00012B/2020